LIFE SKILLS 101:

A Practical Guide to Leaving Home and Living on Your Own

TINA PESTALOZZI

Updated Fifth Edition

STONEWOOD PUBLICATIONS

Publisher's Cataloging-in-Publication

Pestalozzi, Tina.
   Life skills 101 : a practical guide to leaving
home and living on your own / Tina Pestalozzi. —
Fifth Edition
      p. cm.
   Includes bibliographical references and index.
   LCCN: 2010933100
   ISBN: 978-0-9701334-9-6

   1. Life skills. 2. Finance, Personal. 3. Conduct of life. I. Title.

HQ2037.P48 2004   646.7
                                                   QBI00-500070

Printed in the United States of America

Printing History
2001: ISBN 0-9701334-4-8
2004: ISBN 0-9701334-5-6 Second Edition
2007: ISBN 978-0-9701334-7-2 Third Edition
2009: ISBN 978-0-9701334-3-4 Fourth Edition
2011: ISBN 978-0-9701334-9-6 Fifth Edition
2013: ISBN 978-0-9701334-9-6 Fifth Edition, updated

Table of Contents

Introduction

On your own. What do you think of when you read these words? Is living on your own a much anticipated time? Are you looking forward to the day when you will have your own "place?"—when you are responsible for yourself and can live as you please in your own style? Or does the idea of living on your own give you a nervous twinge? Do you feel not quite ready? When are we ready to live on our own anyway?

Of course there is no certain time when we are magically ready to venture out of the nest. Some of us live in circumstances where we feel we've been pretty much on our own for years anyway. For some of us, circumstances dictate that once we hit age eighteen we are out the door, ready or not. Living on your own may mean going away to college. Sometimes it may mean supporting yourself, yet living with a roommate. Living on your own may also mean living with family, but as a self-sufficient, responsible and contributing member of the household.

Whatever your particular age or circumstance, being as prepared as possible makes living on your own an exciting, rather than a difficult, challenge. Having the knowledge and skills required to live successfully alone frees your energy and allows you to grow and fully enjoy the experience. This book is written with the heartfelt intention of both passing along information you may not now know and assembling information you already know into a handy reference to make your new life easier.

There is a tremendous freedom in being a responsible person. Knowing how to easily maneuver through your new world and make it manageable allows you to approach life and receive it at your best. And that is what this book is really all about: acquiring the basic life skills you need to be the best *you* that you can be—to not only survive, but to thrive.

Chapter 1

Stepping into the Working World

Your Dream—Your Plan and Your Present Reality

I graduated from high school knowing I was going to be successful. Yet I had no idea how it was going to happen. None whatsoever. Not only did I not have a clue as to how I would suddenly have the successful life that I envisioned, I basically had no idea of how I was even going to survive. I was on my own and unprepared. "I guess I'll go to work . . . somewhere," I thought. "I'll find something . . . maybe I'll take a few classes somewhere . . . somehow. . . ." Please don't let this happen to you!

I didn't have a plan of how I was going to go about getting where I wanted to be. No matter what point we are at in our lives, having a vision of how we want our lives to be is important. But having the plan, the rough outline, the "road map" of how to get there, is critical.

You must develop a personal plan of how you are actually going to reach your dreams. Outline a plan that will be very easy to follow so that you will stick with it. Just as most of us give up trying to stick to a budget we've made that is too difficult to deal with, you might give up thinking about your plan if you make your road map too complicated. The easiest plan I have seen is the following chart developed by Cynthia Bischoff, a communications trainer. Imagine or visualize your "dream" goal; then divide the steps to reach it into smaller goals. It may help to honestly face facts about your present reality. This will give you an idea of how much you need to do to reach your dream.

Your Dream
Long-Range Goals
Medium-Range Goals
Short-Range Goals
Immediate Action
Your Present Reality

Some people know or think they know at an early age just what they want out of life. Others are not so sure. Once you decide *something* you want to work toward and focus your energy on, you will be giving your life direction. Ideally, you will eventually know and follow the dreams you love. You can count on adjusting your goals as you move forward. You will find yourself adding, subtracting, and moving around your basic life plan. Life is full of irregularities. The old saying, "Expect the unexpected" certainly applies here. We also change our goals as we grow and mature.

Having a life plan can be quite a comfort. You will worry less about your life's direction because you have an idea of where you are going. For instance, you will probably instinctively know if a certain decision is right for you or not. You will ask yourself, "Is this action going to help me reach my goals or keep me further away from making my dreams a reality?" Your life's path will take twists and turns on the way to your dreams. Your dreams may even change several times. Yet accepting complete responsibility for every aspect of your life, including being responsible for your life's direction, is a critical part of being a healthy, whole person, and is also where a great deal of fun and fulfillment lies.

Now, let's look at the chart. You can use this chart not only for your overall life plan, but also to break down any project you tackle. If one of your personal dreams is to see yourself in better shape, toned up with more energy and stamina, use this chart to create a path to reach your goal. If your present reality is that you are out of shape, not eating the right food, too tired even to exercise, your immediate goal may be something small, like eating more fruit and vegetables every day. It doesn't matter how small the action, just faithfully meeting one small goal after another keeps you heading in the right direction.

If living successfully on your own is a dream of yours, what is your present reality? How far are you from your goal? Are you still living at home with plenty of time to calculate your move?

Not every-one has that luxury, but if you do, your plan may look something like this:

Your Plan

Your Dream

To be out of my parent's house and to be living on my own, with at least three months living expenses in my saving account.

Long-Range Goal

Keep my job, or get a better one, and save all I can, even though I'll also be attending college.

Medium-Range Goal

Open a savings and a checking account. Start acquiring as many skills as I need to be employable and marketable.

Short-Range Goal

Get a regular job, or find odd jobs and work part-time while I finish high school.

Immediate Action

Start organizing for my job search.

Your Present Reality

I'm sick of living here, and I can't wait until I'm on my own.

This is a good plan for someone who has the foresight to start thinking and planning early. Yet it's never too late to come up with some sort of plan of action. Whatever your present reality, a little planning and a little knowledge of basic life skills enables you to start living on your own from a position of strength. Ready or not—let's go!

Your Social Skills—Don't Leave Home Without Them

A lot of us grew up acquiring our social skills in a hit-or-miss fashion. Now we make do and hope for the best. We manage to introduce people all the time and get by. We shake hands without giving much thought as to whether we are doing it correctly or not. After all, how much difference can it make? Plenty!

Just as the behavior we would expect from a two-year-old is not appropriate for a nine-year-old, somewhere in our young adult years having immature social skills will no longer be considered acceptable. Many people are technically excellent at their work but fail to achieve the kind of career success they would like because they lack good "people skills." Taking the time to acquire solid personal skills is one of the best investments you can ever make. Start from scratch. Develop an awareness of other people and how your actions appear to them. Respect and consideration for others is the foundation on which all social skills and business etiquette is built. How we treat other people is a direct reflection on us. We are judged, favorably or not, by our actions.

Two of the most helpful books you can read are *Emily Post's Etiquette* and *Letitia Baldrige's New Complete Guide to Executive Manners*. Although the books are really thick, the information and interpersonal skills you will learn can be applied to many areas of your life and make it well worth the reading time. Look for the most current editions. At a minimum, master these few things:

Etiquette Basics

- Respect others
- Shake hands correctly
- Greet people effectively
- Introduce people properly
- Stand for introductions
- Maintain eye contact
- Sound pleasant
- Be aware of others
- Be friendly

Respect Others. The foundation for social skills, etiquette and good manners is respect. It's treating everyone respectfully and operating with mindfulness and awareness about how your behavior is affecting others. We all know what it feels like when we think someone has treated us disrespectfully, so it's easy to see why some version of the **"Golden Rule"** is part of the philosophy of all the major spiritual traditions, and a growing number of corporate and small business cultures, as well.

Shake Hands Correctly. For both men and women a good handshake is firm, connecting the space between your thumb and forefinger with the same space of the hand you are shaking. Be sure not to grab just the fingertips. As well, make sure you don't bend your hand and extend *just* your fingertips. Fully connect and shake, using a gentle up and down motion from the elbow. Be mindful not to squeeze too hard or shake too long. Just two pumps. Do not hesitate in extending your hand. Regardless of gender, shaking hands is the acceptable greeting and should be done again when you say good-bye.

Greet People Effectively. Introduce yourself to people you do not know. Offer your hand, say your name slowly and clearly, and give a little information to help get a conversation going. For example, if you are meeting someone at work, you might say something such as, "Hello, I'm Cris Goode. I just started working in the collections department." It is not correct to ever give *yourself* an honorific title such as Mr., Ms., Mrs., or Dr.

Introduce People Properly. Learn the mechanics of both a business introduction and a social introduction. In business, introductions are based on **precedence,** not gender. You must decide who is considered the more important person in the introduction and present the "lesser" person *to* the "more" important person. This means you would introduce a junior person *to* a senior person. Do this by saying the senior person's name first. For instance, "Ms. Senior, I would like to present *(to you)* Mr. Junior, who is our new intern." You would introduce a peer to your boss, where as your boss would be introduced *to* a client or customer. In social introductions, the older or more distinguished person's name is spoken first, and in most circumstances a man is introduced to a woman.

- In all your introductions, try to be consistent with your use of first names, first and last names, and terms of address, such as Mr. or Ms. You would introduce Mr. Jones to Ms. Smith, David Jones to Jane Smith or David to Jane.

- If you introduce someone by saying "I'd like to introduce my friend. . . ," it sounds as if the other person is not also your friend. Avoid using the expression, *my friend*, in an introduction.

Stand up for Introductions. Whether you are male or female, stand when you are introduced to anyone and everyone. Unless there is a compelling reason for not doing so, such as you are squeezed in a tight spot and your standing would interfere with everyone else, you must always stand for all introductions, even when you hear, "Oh, don't get up."

Maintain Eye Contact. Maintaining good eye contact with the person you are talking to gives the impression that you care what they are saying and that you are respectful. Avoid staring by occasionally looking at another feature of the face.

Sound Pleasant. Don't be lazy in your speech. Whether we like it or not, we are all judged by the way we sound, both in person and on the telephone. Listen to how you sound. Constantly using words such as "like," "you know," and "um" will not be to your best advantage. When you greet someone, say something more than "Hi." "Hello" is better, but "Good Morning, Cari" is even better still.

Be Aware of Others. Be aware of how considerate your behavior is in public. Do you hold open doors for someone who may be approaching behind you? Are you quiet and respectful in public areas? Are you annoying others with your phone conversation? Are you a courteous driver? How we treat people matters. The person you cut off at an intersection today may be the person you face at an employment interview tomorrow.

> Really listening to people is a skill that few fail to appreciate – almost everyone just loves a great listener. This skill alone will help you immensely and when coupled with the practice of never interrupting others, is a sure winner.

Be Friendly. Smile. Be warm. Learn the social skills you need to be comfortable with all people and practice your new skills until you appear at ease wherever you are.

Work—It's a Good Thing

Do you know that many people continue to work long after they no longer financially need to do so? That even some people who by birth or by circumstance never "had" to be employed, still seek out interesting and meaningful work? Work can be a fulfilling aspect of our lives, and for most of us it is essential to our survival as well.

You must have resources to live on your own, and by now you probably realize this most likely means your getting a job, starting your own business, or developing your career. Even while going to college full-time, countless numbers of students must also work at least part-time. At some point, most of us seek out employment, and the following information will help you reach your goal of being successfully employed.

Job Search Success

Presenting yourself at your best is important in all aspects of your employment, but it is critical to your success in seeking a job. From filling out a neat and complete employment application form to sending a thank you note after an interview, you must present yourself in a manner that gives you an edge over your competition. Like it or not, you will be evaluated by the way you handle the process. Try to make a good impression every step of the way.

Organizing for the Job. Be as organized as possible in your job search. Start by gathering together all the information you will need. Know your Social Security number. If you don't have a number, you can apply for one at your local Social Security office or get an application at *www.SocialSecurity.gov.*

If you are under eighteen, you might need to acquire a work permit. Your guidance counselor at school should be able to help you. You can also call your local Labor Department.

You will need three people who are willing to act as references for you. They should not be family members. Make sure you ask permission to include their names, addresses, and phone numbers on your employment application or résumé. Obviously you want to choose someone who you are sure will respond favorably if questioned about you.

Although you may be looking for your first real job, you may already have had some work experience. Have you done volunteer work for a church or community organization? Have you baby-sat for your neighbors or performed yard work? Anyone

Here is guideline information for a first-time basic résumé:

Your name
Your street address
Your city, state and zip code
Your phone number
Your e-mail address

Last grade completed and where

Achievements and awards

Any work experience

Areas of interest or classes you have taken that relate to
the position for which you are applying. Also, list any organizations in which you have been active.

References: Names, addresses, and phone numbers. If you
have listed work experience, have the references listed on a
separate sheet and present them when asked.

Hint: Remember to proofread and check your spelling. Then
have someone else double-check your work.

you have worked for may be a good person to approach for a reference as well as members of the clergy, teachers, or family friends who know you well. If you are looking for your first job, it is appropriate to prepare a résumé with references. If you have an employment history, it is not necessary to include the references in your résumé; but have them ready and with you at an interview in case they are requested.

Résumé: Even if the job you are applying for does not require you to submit a résumé, it is a good idea to prepare one so you will have all the necessary information with you. Your résumé should look as professional as possible, so be sure it is typed on plain white paper. Do not use notebook paper or creative stationery. Your school or local library will have books on how to write an appropriate résumé.

The more positive information you acquire to add to your résumé, the more sophisticated your résumé should become. In addition to being completely accurate, easy to read, and concise, it should also reflect a high standard of presentation.

A common résumé format is reverse-chronological, in which you list your most recent employment experience and work backward through your education and work history. A skills-based résumé emphasizes what you can do and what your qualifications are.

No matter which format you decide will work best for you, make sure the résumé emphasizes your strong points and is written in an active tone, using action verbs such as "arranged," "organized," "tutored," and so forth.

Study samples in résumé-writing guidebooks. Your résumé is the tool you create to market yourself. Work with your résumé until it is as good as it can be and reflects you at your best.

What Job? Chances are good that you will have had some other work experience before you actually find the job that financially allows you to live on your own. Deciding what kind of job or career you want can take time and patience. Thankfully, there are a lot of resources available to you if you need help making your decision. Check with schools and college-career counseling centers in your area.

- If you are starting to look for your first job, have an idea of the type of job you want to apply for. Try to find a job that complements your interests and abilities. For instance, if you enjoy swimming, you might apply for a position as a lifeguard at your local community pool or YMCA. Discuss your plans with your parents or guardians. They may have some ideas about where you should and should not apply for work. Get the word out to relatives and family friends that you are looking for employment. Perhaps you will get a solid lead to follow or a suggestion that you have not thought of. School counselors may provide job leads.

- If you already have the education and/or experience to apply for your "ideal" job, your job search will be more sophisticated, as will your résumé and your interview techniques. Be prepared to discuss your particular strengths and what you can offer. In addition, you can help yourself out by doing as much research as you can about the company to which you are applying. If applicable, review the company's web site and annual report, as well as any articles that have been written about the company.

Appropriate Responses

Say:	Instead of:
Hello	Hi or hey
Good-bye	Bye or See ya
All right	Okay or yeah
Thank you	Thanks
Avoid:	Uh . . . cool . . . like . . . um . . . you know . . . awesome . . .

- Check the "help wanted" section of your local paper. An ad may direct you to call or write. If you call regarding an ad, you should identify yourself and state why you are calling. Make sure you answer all questions in complete sentences.

Cover Letter. Your written request for a job interview is typically called a cover letter when you include a copy of your résumé. With or without a résumé, a letter used to initiate communication with a potential employer should be neat and demonstrate competence. Your letter should be one page and typed on the same type of paper as your résumé.

- Try to limit your letter to three paragraphs. Introduce yourself and tell how you heard about the job opening in the first paragraph. The second paragraph should highlight specific qualifications and skills you can offer. Close with a third paragraph requesting an interview.

The Internet is a terrific resource for information designed to help you decide what educational and career options are right for you. You may want to check out:

www.actstudent.org	*www.adventuresineducation.org*
www.careeronestop.org	*www.careerpath.com*
www.getthatgig.com	*www.mappingyourfuture.org*
www.myfuture.com	*www.stats.bls.gov/k12/index.htm*

For help with an advanced job search you may want to visit:

www.careerbuilder.com	*www.careercast.com*
www.careerlab.com	*www.collegerecruiter.com*
www.indeed.com	*www.jobbankinfo.org*
www.job-hunt.org	*www.monstertrak.com*
www.rileyguide.com	*www.snagajob.com*

Use this example to help you construct your own cover letter:

Your street address
Your city, state and zip code
Phone number
E-mail address

Month, date and year

Contact person's name – Mr. or Ms. – and correct title
(Example: Ms. Jane Doe, Manager)
Name of the company *(Example: Ezings Pizza and Pasta)*
Street address or P.O. Box
City, state, and zip code

Dear Ms. Doe:

In response to your advertisement in the January 7, 2014 edition of the *San Pedro News Pilot,* I would like to be considered for the position of Counter Person.

I am seventeen years old and a junior at San Pedro High School. I am an honor student and I have been recognized by my instructors as being a dependable and hardworking person. I always strive to do my best.

I would like to meet you to discuss my capabilities as they apply to the position with Ezings Pizza and Pasta. I appreciate your time and consideration.

Sincerely,

Your signature

Your first and last name

Enclosure *(If you are enclosing your résumé)*

The Application. For many positions, such as retail sales or working at large grocery stores, you can walk in any time and request an application which you can complete there; or take home, fill out, and return another time. Even if you are just picking up an application, look presentable.

- Do *not* go anywhere to apply for a job or to an interview, without having a pen with you. Make sure you use black or blue ink.

- Neatness, spelling, grammar, and good penmanship are essential.

- Answer every question on the form completely and correctly. When you are finished, check over the application to make sure you have not left any spaces blank. This shows that you have read the application thoroughly. Write "N/A" for "not applicable" if a question does not apply to you.

- Many applications ask for salary requirements. You may wish to write "open." This leaves room for a later salary discussion and possible negotiation.

Hint: It is a good idea to ask to see a job description for the position you are applying for. You do not want to commit yourself to a job if you are not fully aware of exactly what it entails.

You Have an Interview. Whether you are facing your first job interview or have a couple behind you, here are a few pointers to help you navigate the interview process.

Plan ahead for the interview – to arrive a few minutes early with a couple of black or blue ink pens and to be prepared for basic questions you might be asked. Although there are hundreds of possible questions an interviewer may throw out to you, what they are most likely trying to find out is how dependable you are, if you're a hard worker, if you are easy to get along with, and what kind of skills, if any, you can bring to the job. Keep those things in mind as you frame your answers to the questions you are asked. Think ahead how you would answer the questions "Tell me about yourself" or "What are your greatest strengths?"

Once you are fortunate enough to get an interview, remember only a true emergency should keep you from showing up at the scheduled appointment on time. Excuses like, "I couldn't make it because the friend who was going to give me a ride was waiting for her brother to get back from.... etc." will help a potential employer decide you are not the candidate for the job. Sometimes you may be asked to call or return several times before you are told whether or not you have the job. Don't give up, and be sure you follow up, since this may be a test to see how dependable you are and how well you follow instructions.

During your interview, remember attitude is everything. It's why an employer may hire you instead of someone who is just as smart or just as qualified. The proper attitude shows that you are positive and eager to please. It's caring enough not only to be on time, but to arrive several minutes early. It's wanting the job bad enough to make a good impression. Your clothes should be clean, pressed, and appropriate. Mirror, or dress slightly better than, what is worn in the organization at the level you are applying for. Men, now is the time to tuck in your shirt and put on a tie. Women, dress conservatively. Forget about wearing faded or torn jeans, T-shirts, tank tops or shorts. Nails need to be neat. Shoes should be shined. Every part of you needs to be clean and look well-groomed and well put together. You are projecting how you feel about yourself by the way you dress and present yourself.

- It may seem hard to appear relaxed yet energetic at the same time, but you can do it. Greet your interviewer properly:
  - ✓ Introducing yourself by using both your first and last names
  - ✓ Smile
  - ✓ Extend a greeting (such as "thank you for seeing me")
  - ✓ Shake hands correctly
  - ✓ Use direct eye contact
  - ✓ Watch your posture

Interview Don'ts:

- Slump
- Fidget
- Interrupt
- Stare
- Talk to the floor
- Check your watch
- Chew gum
- Crack your knuckles
- Fiddle with your hair
- Play with your hands, cuticles, ring, necklace, and so on.

- Maintain good direct eye contact during your interview. This indicates you are focused and interested. Do not stare; just appear to be listening and friendly.
- Sit when you are instructed to do so. Don't slump, fidget, play with your hands, cross your legs, or tap your feet. Just sit up straight in the chair with your feet flat on the floor.
- Be mindful not to interrupt.
- Answer all questions completely and honestly. Don't say you have experience if you do not. Don't say you know how to do something if you know you don't. Never lie. Answer all questions in complete sentences which will help to keep you from appearing indifferent.
- Show interest! During the interview you may wish to ask questions such as:
  - ✓ What would my duties be during a typical workday?
  - ✓ Will I be working with others or by myself?
  - ✓ What type of promotions are available from the position?

- Try to emphasize your dependability and your willingness to work hard.
- Discuss your strengths, skills, and accomplishments, not how much money you want. Let the interviewer bring up salary, even if it's approached in a subsequent interview.
- When the interview is over, make sure you smile, shake hands again, and say thank you. Immediately after the interview write and send, via e-mail or postal mail, a short, well-written letter thanking the interviewer for the time given you and restating your interest in the position. This is an additional opportunity to impress the interviewer and to project the positive attitude employers are looking for.

Workplace Savvy

A major part of your life will be spent working. Your job will be important to you on many levels, and hopefully it will give you the financial support you need. Yet, the satisfaction that you can obtain from enjoying your job and performing it well may mean just as much to you as the financial rewards it offers.

You show a great deal about who you are in your approach to your work. Demonstrate that you respect yourself enough to honor your commitment to your job. Be willing to give it your best. Be willing to work. Be happy to be useful. Make sure you are never late. Being late must never be more than a rare occurrence. Show that you are both dependable and responsible.

- Be courteous. Are you pleasant to work with? Are your co-workers happy to spend time with you? Look carefully at your behavior in the workplace. Employers want employees who can get along with everyone and are cheerful to be around. Never put people down in front of others. Do not engage in mean gossip or allow others to gossip to you. Keep your promises and your confidences.

- Find out about the dress code before you begin your new job and make sure you continue to dress appropriately. Suggestive or revealing clothes are not for the workplace. Dress the way the person responsible for your promotions expects you to dress.

- When you are new to the workplace, you may find that you need to adjust how you manage your time. Develop the habit of planning ahead; for instance, make sure your work clothes are clean and that you have gas in your car.

  You may find you need to change a few old habits, like staying out late on a work night, or that you need to start a few new routines, such as using a daily planner to keep track of things you need to remember. Take the necessary actions to remain organized and to adjust to your new responsibilities.

- Make it a habit to think before you speak. Communicate as clearly as you can and always speak with respect.

- Develop your listening skills. Being a good listener can greatly contribute to your on-the-job success.

- Approach every job and job challenge as an opportunity to increase your skills.

- Whatever your job, remember that there is dignity in work, and great satisfaction can be gained from knowing you do your particular job well and give your best.

The Value of Networking

We are all connected to each other. The way we treat each other matters. There's an old saying, "You never know to whom you're talking." Not only does this apply to being careful of what you say to whom, but it is very true about people and their connections. Making a good impression on someone, projecting competence, and being thought of favorably may be a huge asset to your long-range plans. Perhaps you will someday be in business for yourself and the contacts you make now will be beneficial to you. Perhaps the friend of an acquaintance will some day be just the person with the experience you need to give you expert advice. We grow as individuals when we keep an expanding circle of acquaintances. Your genuine interest in others and a natural kindness to everyone has its own rewards.

Related Reading

Career Match: Connecting Who You Are with What You'll Love to Do by Shoya Zichy and Ann Bidou. AMACOM; 2007.

Do What You Are: Discover the Perfect Career for You Through the Secrets of Personality Type by Paul D. Tieger and Barbara Barron. Little, Brown and Company; 2007.

Fast Start Success Skills for Tomorrow's Young Professional by Tina Pestalozzi and Natalya Pestalozzi. Stonewood Publications; 2014.

Get Hired: Using Social Media Networks to Land a Job by John Alexander. Quite Right Publications; 2012.

The Job-Hunter's Survival Guide: How to Find a Rewarding Job Even When "There Are No Jobs" by Richard N. Bolles. Ten Speed Press; 2009.

Networking for People Who Hate Networking: A Field Guide for Introverts, the Overwhelmed, and the Underconnected by Devora Zack. Berrett-Koehler Publishers; 2010.

Now What?: The Young Person's Guide to Choosing the Perfect Career by Nicholas Lore. Fireside; 2008.

The Pathfinder: How to Choose or Change Your Career for a Lifetime of Satisfaction and Success by Nicholas Lore. Touchstone; Revised Updated edition; 2012.

StrengthsFinder 2.0: A New and Upgraded Edition of the Online Test from Gallup's Now, Discover Your Strengths by Tom Rath. Gallup Press; 2007.

Take the Stairs: Seven Steps to Achieving True Success by Rory Vaden. Perigee Trade; 2012.

What Color Is Your Parachute? 2013: A Practical Manual for Job-Hunters and Career-Changers by Richard N. Bolles. Ten Speed Press; 2012.

Chapter 2

Taking Care of Business

Your Official Documents

You have probably already found out that there is a bit of official business you have to take care of in order to function smoothly in our society. The few paper documents that you should obtain now are just the beginning of many "paper valuables" you will collect in your lifetime. You will need to decide how you can best protect them, so you won't have to experience the waste of time and the inconvenience of replacing everything unnecessarily.

Safe Spot. Try to keep everything together. If you decide to keep your papers at home, you can create an "Important Papers" file or folder. In the event of an emergency, it is more likely you could locate your file quickly, than all the separate things it should contain. An accordion-type file folder, a plastic document pouch file, or even a manilla envelope, will keep everything contained and organized. Better yet is a strongbox, which is a fire-proof box designed to survive most fires. They are available at office supply and discount stores. You can also put other valuables in your box. Where to put the box becomes another concern, since you want to make it as difficult as possible to be stolen. As you gain more valuables and obtain more important documents, you may wish to consider getting a safe-deposit box at your bank.

If you are lucky enough to find a bank that offers a free safe-deposit box with a free or low-fee checking or savings account, sign up! The following is a sample list of what your safe-deposit box or strongbox may eventually include:

Paper Valuables

- Birth certificate, original or certified copy
- Contracts
- Diplomas
- Home inventory, including receipts for big purchases and appraisals
- Insurance policies, with customer service phone numbers
- Legal contracts or documents such as marriage or divorce papers
- Master list of your financial accounts and credit card numbers, with the customer service phone number of each provider
- Military papers
- Naturalization papers
- Passport
- Savings bonds
- Social Security card
- Title to your car, deeds, or other records of ownership

Your Will. Whether you want to or not, at some point, you need to prepare your will. There are strict rules concerning wills, and it is best to do a little research before you start. You need to keep your will updated as you acquire more assets. When you have children, you should name in your will who you desire to be their guardians. (Don't let it be a surprise. Be sure to talk it over beforehand with the person(s) you select). Please remember your *original* will is the one thing that does *not* belong in your safe-deposit box. Most states "seal" (limit access to) your safe-deposit box at the time of death. Original wills should ideally be left in the care of a law office. You can keep your original will in a safe spot at home, but you may also wish to give it to a trusted friend or family member, especially one with a safe-deposit box!

Birth Certificate. Obtaining this document first will make acquiring other documents you may need a lot easier. You should have at least one *certified* copy of your birth certificate. This differs from a regular copy in that it has an official stamp or certification. Birth certificates are kept by the county of the state where you were born. Check the phone book or directory assistance for the number of the Office of Vital Statistics. The offices that keep the records are listed under various names nationwide, but generally fall under the jurisdiction of the Health Department. Fees for each copy vary. To obtain your birth certificate online, visit the National Center for Health Statistics: *www.cdc.gov/nchs.*

Photo Identification. This usually takes the form of a driver's license. If for any reason you do not drive, it is still possible to get official photo identification from your local Department or Bureau of Motor Vehicles. Call your local office to find out what the requirements are.

Driver's License. This falls under the jurisdiction of the state where you live, and requirements vary from state to state. Remember to keep the address on your license current. You will also need to get a new driver's license if you change your state of residence.

Vehicle Registration. The Department or Bureau of Motor Vehicles is also where you register your vehicle. There is a fee to pay every year to keep your registration current. Depending on your state's requirements, you may be asked to present verification that your vehicle meets your state's emission standards. You will be told if you need the certification when you register and where you can obtain it.

If you sell or give away your vehicle, it is very important to complete the necessary paperwork with the Department or Bureau of Motor Vehicles *immediately.* The record of the transaction must be on file with your state, so in the event of an accident, parking tickets, or other law infractions by the new owners, you are free from liability.

Vehicle Title. A title to a car is the document that shows ownership. If you buy a car and pay cash for it, you will receive the title, which you must take to your local title office and have recorded. If you get a loan from a bank to buy the car, the title has a **lien** placed on it from the bank. When the loan is paid off, the lien is removed, and you receive a clear title. You may also record a change in title when you change states and register your car in your new state. If you do not know where to record titles in your area, call your local Department or Bureau of Motor Vehicles.

Voter Registration. If you want to vote in any election, generally you must register in advance. Call your local Board of Elections to find out what identification you need to bring with you when you register.

> **Hint:** Visit *www.USA.gov*, the U.S. government's official web portal, when you need answers to a government related question. With a wide range of topics, it's a great place to start a search for official government listings, services, and other related resources.

Social Security Card. You can't go very long without having your own Social Security number. Hospitals provide applications for numbers to parents of newborns. Chances are your parents obtained your number for you when you were very young in order to declare you as a dependent on their income tax. In the event that you do not yet have a Social Security number, visit the Social Security Administration's web site at *www.SocialSecurity.gov*. There you can download an application and determine the documents you'll need to accompany your application to prove your identity, age, and citizenship or lawful alien status. All documents will need to be either originals or copies certified by the issuing agency. You can also check the site for the location of your nearest Social Security office where you can apply in person for your card.

The Social Security system has been in effect since 1935 to help provide old age benefits to retired workers and their dependents and to help provide for the disabled. The Social Security Administration (SSA) identifies you and tracks your lifetime earnings by the number they issue to you. Your employers need to know your correct number as does the Internal Revenue Service (IRS). It is very important to protect the privacy of your number. Identity theft is one of the fastest growing crimes in America. It's real and can be a nightmare. One example of identity theft is if someone uses your Social Security number to obtain a credit card in their name. This can potentially ruin your good credit record.

Protect your Social Security number. Make it your policy not to give out your number automatically, but to carefully consider every request and to be selective as to who receives it. For instance, your bank needs to know your number to report interest earned on your accounts to the IRS, but a local business can identify you by some other means. You should always ask why your number is needed, how it will be used and what will happen if you refuse. The answers to these questions can help you decide if you want to give out your number. Use your best judgment here. Release the number only when absolutely necessary and make sure you never have your Social Security number printed on your bank checks.

- To ensure you are credited with your correct earnings, be sure you notify the SSA if you change your name. You will need to show proof both of your old name and your new name. You will get a new card in your new name with your old number.

- If you are 25 years of age or older, use a "my Social Security" online account at *www.SocialSecurity.gov* to get your Social Security Statement. This report estimates your retirement, disability, and survivors benefits; shows your earnings record and the estimated Social Security and Medicare taxes you've paid.

- Memorize your number and keep the card in a safe place. While you normally should not carry it in your wallet where it can easily be lost or stolen, do not rely on your memory for furnishing the number on important documents, such as those involving your employment.

- Don't use the last four digits of your number as your secret PIN (Personal Identification Number) on any of your financial accounts.

- Shred any document that has your Social Security number on it before you throw it away.

- Call the SSA at *800.772.1213* or visit their web site at *www.SocialSecurity.gov* if you have any questions or if you would like the address of your local Social Security office and its hours of operation. You can also request factsheets, including "Identity Theft and Your Social Security Number," Publication No. 05–10064.

Passport. A passport is only a necessity if you are planning to travel out of the country. Otherwise it is just an excellent source of identification and a comfort to know you have in case an unexpected opportunity arises; then you're ready to go. You can apply for your passport at many post offices, county/municipal offices, and federal and state courts. Passports come under the jurisdiction of the U.S. Department of State; Bureau of Consular Affairs. (*www.state.gov*) For complete information, including a list of the documents you need to submit and the location of a passport agency or acceptance facility near you, call the National Passport Information Center at *877.487.2778* or visit *http:// travel.state.gov/passport.* Generally you will need:

1. *Form DS-11: Application for Passport.* You may pick the form up at the facility and return it later, but you must sign this form *in person* at the passport acceptance facility.

2. *Proof of U.S. Citizenship.* Proof could be your certified birth certificate or your naturalization certificate.

3. *Proof of Identity.* Such proof could be a current, valid driver's license or current school ID card.

4. *The Fee.* The current fee is listed on the application. Depending on how and where you apply, the accepted methods of payment vary, so be sure to find out ahead of time.

5. *One Passport Photograph.* The photo must be recent, in color, printed on photo quality paper and 2" x 2" in size. Check *www.travel.state.gov/passport* for additional requirements.

The State Department recommends applying for your passport several months before your departure date. Your passport will be mailed to the address you put on the application, about 25 days after your application is received. It is possible to get your passport issued faster, but you must pay an additional fee to expedite the process.

The Department of State also issues the U.S. Passport Card as a less expensive, alternative to the traditional passport book. However, the card cannot be used for travel by air. It is valid for land and sea crossings between the U.S. and Canada, Mexico, the Caribbean and Bermuda only.

> If you've caught the travel bug and are thinking about having an adventure outside of the U.S., take a look at *www.studentsabroad.state.gov.* Here you'll find everything you need to know from the U.S. Department of State about how to prepare for, stay legal, and return safely from your travels abroad.

Other Licenses and Permits. When I moved from a large city to a small town, I was very surprised to find out I needed a permit to hold a garage sale. Every state, city, and town has different laws and ordinances, and it's a good idea to find out what is required in your area before the event. When in doubt, check with local officials on things such as:

Licenses and Permits

Bikes of any kind

Block parties

Building or remodeling

Burning (leaves, yard waste, construction waste, trash, etc.)

Conducting a business in your home

Dogs; farm, exotic, or other animals

Fishing

Guns

Hunting

Marriage

Sales of any kind (garage, yard, tag, bake, book, etc.)

Street and/or overnight parking (especially of recreational vehicles)

Your Mail

The U.S. Postal Service delivers over 160 billion pieces of mail every year, yet it is still able to provide you with individual service, such as holding your mail upon request. Small towns may only have one post office, but larger cities may have several. "Your" post office is the one that handles your zip code. This is the office where you would pick up anything that the mail carrier was unable to deliver to your address, such as a registered letter or package that required a signature and you were not available when the carrier attempted delivery. It is not necessarily the post office closest to where you live. "Your" post office is also the office that will hold your mail when needed. Just fill out the appropriate form from the post office and your mail will be held on the dates you request. You can indicate on the form if you are going to pick it up or if you want it all delivered to your address on a specific date. When you fill out a change of address card your first class mail will be forwarded to your new address. Make sure you notify everyone who sends you mail of your new address. Magazines usually need six to eight weeks notice before the change becomes effective. Most post offices also provide many other services as well, such as selling money orders and handling passport applications.

- The U.S. Postal Service has a 24-hour phone line for general information on post office locations, hours, zip codes, and mailing rates: *800.275.8777*. Their web site is *www.usps.com*.

Your Taxes

The following information is a basic overview to help give you a general idea of your tax responsibilities. The time to start thinking about your taxes is the time you start having income or start planning a business. Income is not only money you make through your efforts, like your salary and/or tips, but may also be money you make from many other sources, such as **interest** or **dividends** on investments, or be such things as gifts, goods or services. When your **gross income** reaches a specific amount (the exact amount can be different each tax year), you may be required to file a **tax return**. You must keep track of your finances to determine what year you need to start filing a tax return and to know what tax form is right for your circumstances. Visit the Internal Revenue Service's web site at *www.IRS.gov*. or call the Internal Revenue Tax Form request number (*800.829.3676*) to obtain Publication number 17—*Your Federal Income Tax*. This free publication will tell you more than you ever want to know about your taxes and what forms are best for your situation.

When you figure your tax form, you will determine if you owe the U.S. Treasury any money or if the Treasury owes you a refund. During the year, your employer typically takes out a set amount from your paycheck every pay period. This amount is determined by the **withholding** information you provided on your **W-4 form** when you were hired. You may find the amount taken out was too much (and you get a refund), or you may need to write a check to the U.S. Treasury for the difference between what was taken out of your wages by your employer (or paid) and what you owe.

Record Keeping. You may earn money without having money taken out for taxes. This does not mean you do not have to consider it income. You do! If you have income from a source such as your own small business, your record keeping should be especially detailed. Save receipts for everything, and don't be careless with any documentation.

- Federal personal income tax returns must be filed every year by mid-April, usually the 15th. Filing your own return may not be too difficult or too time-consuming, but it really helps to be prepared for the job. Do yourself a big favor and keep accurate records from the beginning of your earning history. Create a system to keep everything together. You need to keep documentation of any income, such as your current cumulative pay stub, and documentation of any **deductions** you may claim, such as cancelled checks *and* receipts. You may receive a **W-2 form** from your employer. This should be provided to you no later than January 31st of the current year. You will also receive Form 1099 from your financial institution if you have interest or dividends that have been reported to the IRS.

- Order IRS Publication number 552—*Recordkeeping for Individuals*. It explains exactly which records you should have and how long to keep them. Hang on to everything for at least three years (seven years if you want to be absolutely sure). Normally, if you are going to be audited (this is when the IRS takes a closer look at your return), it would be before the time limit (**period** or **statute of limitations**) for the return expires. Keep in mind the statute of limitations does not apply if you have filed a fraudulent return or if you did not file when you were required to do so.

- There are plenty of resources available to help you with your taxes, including the IRS who will try to answer any questions you may have. The number for IRS assistance is *800.829.1040.*

- **Tax schedules** are separate forms that may need to be filed along with your return. Visit *www.IRS.gov* to request or view tax schedules, forms and/or publications online. Forms can be downloaded, faxed, or mailed. Common forms, publications and tax schedules may also be available at your local tax office, post office, or library.

- Online and software tax programs are designed to help make filing your year-end return easy and accurate. You might want to check out the free programs at *www.TaxAct.com* and *www.TurboTax.intuit.com*, and also the IRS "Free File" information at *www.irs.gov/uac/Free-File:-Do-Your-Federal-Taxes-for-Free.*

- If you decide you cannot figure your taxes yourself and want professional help, ask around for referrals from people you know who have had successful experiences with tax preparers. If you must pay someone to do your taxes, make sure you do as much as possible ahead of time. You do not want to pay an accountant by the hour to categorize receipts and add up totals that you can do yourself.

- Do not forget about your state taxes. You must figure out your federal return first, then your state return. These forms are also available at your local post office, library, or tax office.

- Make and keep a copy of every tax return (local, state, and federal) you file. They may be useful in helping you prepare future tax returns or if you need to amend (change) a return you have already filed. Tax returns are sometimes requested when applying for loans.

For more free tips, resources and how-to information please visit *www.LifeSkills101.com.*

Chapter 3

Gaining Financial Know-How

Starting Smart

You need financial knowledge to take positive financial actions. The little things you do with your money matter. Cumulatively, a fortune will flow your way during the course of your lifetime. How much of it will you keep? How much will you let flow away? Will you be able to support the lifestyle you dream about? Do you have a financial plan? The more knowledge you acquire, the better your money management skills will be.

The following is general information designed to help you start thinking about your personal financial strategy. It is just one way to go about handling your money. As you gain more money management skills you will find what actions serve you best. We all want to be on solid financial ground. You may not earn much with your first job. You may find it's hard to save a dime. That's the way most of us started out. You may be attending college, receiving financial assistance, and find you have a hard time making ends meet. Don't lose your motivation. Remember, it is possible to meet your financial goals, even moving at a snail's pace—just gain the financial knowledge and trust your instincts.

Know Financial Terms. Familiarize yourself with the following:

> *Certificate of Deposit* (CD)—A savings certificate issued by a bank, credit union, or savings and loan, which allows you to receive interest on the amount of your deposit. The interest rate is determined not only by the amount

deposited, but also by the length of time you agree to keep the funds deposited. You will be penalized if you remove funds before this maturity date.

Exchange-Traded Fund (ETF) —These securities are a variation of the mutual fund, however they trade like a stock throughout the day. They generally have lower costs than the average mutual fund. You purchase ETFs from a brokerage account

Money Market—A deposit account that generally requires a minimum balance, pays a slightly higher rate of interest than a traditional checking account, and allows you to write a limited amount of checks per month. Mutual fund money market accounts usually offer unlimited check writing privileges, but are not insured by the federal government.

Mutual Funds—Investment companies pool the money of small investors into a fund which is managed by a professional fund manager who buys and sells stocks and bonds, and so forth. Every investor owns shares of the fund in proportion to their investment. Make sure you read and understand the funds **prospectus** (facts and terms) before you invest. A mutual fund with a *load* requires a fee to purchase it, a *no-load* mutual fund does not.

Traditional savings account—An account that typically pays a low interest rate, but does not require a high minimum amount to open. It is insured by the U.S. government up to $250,000.

U.S. Savings Bonds—Buying a savings bond is like lending money to the government. Bonds can be purchased at most banks and credit unions. Electronic bonds can be purchased directly from the government at *www. treasurydirect.gov* for as little as $25. Learn about both kinds.

U.S. Treasury Bills, Notes, Bonds and TIPS—These are U.S. government **securities** and are considered the safest of all debt instruments. Treasury bills are currently issued for periods of a few days to fifty-two weeks; notes for two, three, five, seven, or ten years; and bonds for thirty years. TIPS, or Treasury Inflation-Protected Securities, are designed to offer protection against inflation. The minimum purchase price for any of these securities is $100. You can obtain more information by contacting the Bureau of Public Debt Online—*www.treasurydirect.gov.* or by calling Treasury Direct at *800.722.2678.*

Also understand the difference between the following:

Bank—A business that is designed to offer its customers savings and checking accounts, credit, and loans and negotiable securities issued by the government or by a corporation. There are three kinds of banks: commercial banks, savings banks, and savings and loans.

Credit Union—A group of individuals having something in common (such as a religious organization, labor union, or employees of a company) form a not-for-profit financial institution. A credit union may offer a full range of services, generally paying higher interest rates on deposits to its customers and charging lower interest rates on loans than a commercial bank or savings and loan association.

Brokerage Firm (or brokerage house)—A business that helps you exchange securities, such as stocks and bonds or mutual funds. There are full-service brokers who give advice on picking investments and planning your financial strategy; and discount brokers who charge lower commissions than full-service brokers, but give little, if any, advice.

Creating Your Financial Plan

Did you know just what you were going to do with your first paycheck? Did you buy something or did you save it, or a combination of both? You need to know exactly what to do with your money coming in. You also need to be comfortable with the decisions you make. For instance, you do not want to be so strict with yourself about not spending *any* money, that you break down and make an extravagant purchase because you feel deprived. You need a plan, but it needs to be a plan that takes into consideration who you are, your responsibilities, and what you can reasonably expect from yourself.

You notice I am not saying *budget*. I am not going to tell you to make up a budget because I don't know anyone who successfully follows one his whole lifetime. I am telling you to be absolutely aware and totally conscious of exactly how you manage your money. Make it a life-long habit to be in control of your money. You choose how to earn it, save it, spend it, and build security for yourself and those you love.

I want you to formulate your own plan according to your own needs. Remember the life goal chart in Chapter 1? After reading through the nine positive actions I'm going to suggest, please use the chart again, this time to organize your financial goals. I recommend that you structure your plan around the following:

Positive Financial Actions

- Make money.
- Live debt free.
- Always pay yourself first.
- Be accountable to yourself for your spending habits.
- Establish an emergency fund.
- Establish a short-term savings account.
- Establish a wealth investment account.
- Always use your credit cards responsibly.
- Establish a retirement account as early as possible.

In addition to being conscious actions, these suggestions are also long-term positive habits. It doesn't matter if you are not able to start all nine at once. What does matter is that you are developing a long-term personal commitment to your positive financial future.

Make Money. Before you think "make money" is too obvious a thing to say, consider this: There is a big difference between someone who knows they need to make money and someone who internalizes and acts on that idea. You can live well by making money. You can get wealthy by making money. You can significantly help others when you make money. Perhaps all of us to one degree or another secretly wish for a money miracle – but a wish, as they say, is not a plan. A lottery ticket is a pretty crummy plan. Hitching your cart to someone else's star is also not a very good plan. *Making money* can be *your* plan – and it can be a great one.

When you don't have enough money, it's time to accept responsibility and use your energy, knowledge and skills to set things right. Yes, you may need to make some immediate changes to live within your limited means. Yet, you don't ever want to get stuck focusing there. You also need to activate the *mindset* that sets things straight by making more money – by adding more cash. Then the really interesting and exciting work begins as you manage your new money well – even eventually using it to create more cash producing assets!

As a young person just starting out you may already be doing all that you can to generate income, get an education, and gain valuable skills. One day your future, older self is going to be very grateful for the hard work you've put in laying the foundation of your solid financial future. Having a 'make money' mindset is not only about taking care of yourself now, but also about positioning yourself for a better life as you age. For many reasons, people all too often give up and resign themselves to their current level of life circumstances. They may believe they are powerless to move forward. They may believe that things are somehow just going to change for the better without actually having to make that change happen. They may sincerely believe that they live without opportunity. Or they just may not want to take on that extra job or start a business on the side. Yet, if you commit to a make money mindset, you are resolved that no matter what the external circumstances around you may be, you will choose to act in your own best interest, keep going, earn and create the money that you want and need in order to accomplish your financial and life goals.

Live Debt Free. I believe your life will never truly be your own as long as you are harnessed to a burden of debt. Owing money is a burden, no matter if you owe an institution, such as a bank or credit card company, or if you owe a friend or relative. Even if you have an interest-free loan (like from Mom or Dad), debt can mentally and emotionally wear you down.

Respect yourself and your financial game plan enough to make decisions that will take you toward meeting your goals, not move you backward. Having debt is going backward. When you take out a loan, you are charged interest for the use of the money you borrow. When you pay interest, you are not only losing that amount, you are also losing the amount your money would earn if it were working for you, as in an investment. It is not uncommon to still be paying on a loan for a purchase when the item you bought has long since broke or is no longer important in your life.

Before you take on any debt, I suggest you ask yourself, "Is what I want to purchase truly worth the obligation?" For example, is that particular brand new car you can't stop thinking about really worth five years of monthly payments? *Every* month? No exceptions?

You will take on debt in your life. We all do. A home mortgage is generally considered an acceptable form of debt. We all know it is going to cost us something every month for shelter whether we rent or buy. Student loans may be considered tolerable obligations because hopefully the education we receive will help get us get a better job and salary. Few people are fortunate enough to be in the position to pay cash for their car, and so take on an auto loan out of necessity for transportation. There are logical reasons for taking on debt, but maintain the mindset to obligate yourself to debt *only* if it is in your overall best interest; assume the least amount possible and pay it back as quickly as you can. I suggest you seriously think about and research the *true* cost of any debt you want to take on. Know exactly how much interest you will end up paying. Is the payment so high it will interfere with your savings plan? Would you be better off financing a less expensive vehicle that is just as reliable? Would you be better off investing what you would save by having a lower payment?

Staying debt-free requires determination. You will be tempted. You will make tough choices. Yet the rewards of a debt-free lifestyle more than compensate for the challenge.

Always Pay Yourself First. If you are like most people, you tell yourself, "If there is anything left over at the end of the month, I'll try to put it in my savings account." In much the same unexplainable way as how our earthly possessions take on a life of their own and expand to fill every empty space we have to store them, money also seems to have a life of its own and tries to keep flowing out, in spite of what our intentions for it may be.

One way to deal with our outflowing money is to grab it at its source. Take your savings first! There will never be enough left over. No matter how much money you make, if you are like the rest of us, you will be inclined to spend more. Develop the lifelong habit of taking a certain amount right off the top of any money that comes in. Once you have regular earnings, you may want to consider setting up an automatic deposit from your checking account straight into your savings. The old rule of thumb is to save at least ten percent every pay period. If you are working, but do not yet have the financial responsibilities of living on your own, perhaps you can save a much larger percent. You can adjust that amount, taking into consideration what your personal goals are and how fast you intend to reach them. It is the habit of consistently adding to your savings that is important here. Don't put it off. Do you know people who pass up a gourmet cup of coffee because they want to save the money, then drive to the bank to deposit the two dollars they saved? Of course not. Don't give *all* your money the chance to flow out. Paying yourself first assures that you save *something,* and a little something over time helps build your financial independence.

Be Accountable to Yourself for Your Spending Habits.
Have you ever thought you had more money in your wallet or
purse than you did? Did you have a hard time trying to remember what in the world you spent the missing money on? Inatten-
tion to our spending is another area that trips us up.

While it would drive you crazy to account for every single
cent you spend, you do need to have an accurate idea of where
your money is going. Is the amount you are spending every
month on target with your financial game plan? Do you recognize your spending habits? If you feel bad, do you regularly buy
yourself something to cheer yourself up? Are you an impulse
shopper? Do you give yourself convincing little lectures on why
it's okay to buy something now when you know darn well you
really should wait?

Some people are better at watching their pennies than others, but most people spend more money every month than they
realize. This is where the danger starts. Benjamin Franklin had
it right when he said, "Beware of little expenses; a small leak
will sink a great ship." It's hard to visualize how saving on little
things can make a significant difference to your long-range financial goals. It's also hard to remain committed and motivated to
stick to being accountable for how you spend your money. Make
up your mind to remain motivated to stick to your financial game
plan. Even a small thing like eating lunch out every day can affect your long-term financial picture. Maybe you've heard you can
save hundreds of dollars every year by brown bagging your lunch.
It's true. This may be an area where you can save money. Yet the
decision to pack your lunch is just one example of the attention,
the mindset, and the conviction it is going to take for you to live
within your means and to be true to your financial plan. It also
requires a daily consciousness about your goals and what you do
with your cash. How important to you is your financial independence? Will you take your financial game plan seriously? Every
day you will be required to commit yourself again to your financial
future. Every expenditure requires thought.

The need to be aware of how you are spending your money
doesn't go away when you start making more. Your financial
portfolio will change, but the necessity of spending your money

wisely does not. No matter how much money you have, you will still be accountable, at least to yourself, for your spending. I'm not suggesting you turn yourself into a real cheapskate. Just keep in mind you will need to act responsibly, not only for the rent and the car payment, but also for the extras like magazines, music downloads, apps. and those huge buckets of popcorn at the movies. The little totals do add up.

Another danger, of course, is in thinking you've been so good at saving on the little things that you make a huge purchase you are not ready for. Be careful of those big ticket items! The wrong one at the wrong time may throw you financially off balance. Meeting your financial goals is too important not to give every purchase the consideration it deserves. You are accountable to you. Just pay attention to both the small and the large expenditures, and you won't have to answer to yourself for messing up.

Establish an Emergency Fund. You know you need a savings account. You should also have money set aside in an emergency account. This means, of course, for emergencies *only*. It is not the money you use when your friend wants you to go along on a spur of the moment vacation to Aruba. It is the money you have set aside for *when,* not *if,* unexpected expenses come up. And they will. Cars break down. You may get sick and miss a lot of work. You may even lose your job. Having this safety net in place may mean the difference between being able to meet your rent or having to move.

Ideally, if you have not yet set out on your own, you should try to make sure your emergency fund is in place before you move. Estimates vary, but it is generally recommended you have from three to six months living expenses saved. This means you figure out how much you will need every month just to get by (include everything: rent, utilities, food, gas, etc.) and multiply it by the number of months you want to have in reserve. Sounds like a lot, doesn't it? Make sure you have at *least* three months worth of expenses set aside. After that, guess what? *Then* you can actually start saving to move out. Yes, only after you have enough put away for emergencies can you even begin to think about saving to move out.

You notice I said ideally. Perhaps you are already on your own, struggling just to pay the rent. Whatever your circumstances, make funding an emergency account a priority—even if you have to take on a second job temporarily to come up with the money. It's that important. Here's why. In addition to wanting to be prepared for an emergency, you are also going to need to build a solid financial future. Part of that process involves saving and investing. You will not be able to invest effectively if you have to take money away from your investments to cover life's surprise expenses. It is very hard to build a solid financial future without benefiting from solid investing. Investing just a few dollars regularly helps you tremendously over time. Having to interrupt your investment strategy may end up costing you more than you realize.

Once you are on your own, an important thing to remember about an emergency account is to make sure you can get to the money without delay and/or penalties. With some savings vehicles, such as certificates of deposits (CDs), you will be penalized if you make a withdrawal before the agreed-upon time has passed. If this is all the money you have, don't tie up the entire amount.

Another consideration is that you may not want to keep such a large amount of money in your checking account or regular savings account that pays you a very low interest rate. One reasonable option may be to have your emergency fund in a money market account. Money market accounts generally pay more than a regular savings account, and you can get to your money whenever you need it. You are allowed a limited number of transactions per month, which you hopefully will not need anyway. Generally, a minimum amount is required to open a money market account, so you may need to plan accordingly. Money market accounts that are insured by the government are available at many traditional financial institutions such as banks, savings and loan associations, and credit unions. There is a similar fund called a money market mutual fund. This is a type of mutual fund, and it is *not* insured by the government. There is a difference. If you open a mutual fund money market account, I suggest you use a large and well-known fund. Make sure you read and understand all of the available information on the fund.

When you are living on your own and you have more than six months' living expenses set aside, you may want to spread the money over a couple of different accounts. Perhaps use both a money market fund and a short-term CD. Wherever you decide to put your emergency fund, knowing you have a safety net to fall back on will give you peace of mind. It will also play an important part in your saving and investment strategy. As you prepare to step out on your own, an emergency fund should be one of your top priorities.

Establish a Short-Term Savings Account. A short-term savings account is for saving up for the near and sort-of-near future. It is better than having a stash around the house because you cannot get to it on a second's impulse and because you can put the money somewhere that pays you interest, or a return, on what you deposit. I believe saving up and paying cash for a purchase is always best. (Using a credit card to make the purchase is fine, but don't buy the item unless you already have the money set aside and can pay the credit card balance when it arrives.) This is the account you use to save to meet those not-too-distant goals. This is where you park the money that you are hiding from yourself. Remember that ten percent rule from "Pay Yourself First?" You may want to divide part of the amount you decided to save into a short-term and part into a long-term account.

Make it easy on yourself to save. Those who do better at consistently saving are those who automate the process and use automatic payments, such as from a checking account into a savings account at regular intervals. Use whatever method of saving that works best for you. It's the development of the habit of systematic saving that is so important here.

Establish a Wealth Investment Account: Did you notice I used the term "investment" here and not "savings"? Investing is taking your capital (money) and using it in a way in which you expect to gain more capital or income in the future. Think of this account as being your wealth creation account. You will use this money to make more money—by investing in such a way that you will create and grow money. Even if you can only set aside a few dollars a month, set up an automatic payment to this account as soon as possible. Using both your youth and your dedication to your financial game plan to your advantage, you can certainly obtain financial independence and enjoy security for yourself and those you love.

Being ready to start investing means not only do you need to have some dollars available for investing, but that you have also educated yourself on what types of investment opportunities are right for you. Since investing involves a level of risk, some people are more comfortable putting their money in traditional savings accounts or in securities issued by the U.S. government. They may need the peace of mind of knowing their money is insured by the **full faith and credit** of the government. However, *true investing* offers the potential for the greatest return. Educate yourself as thoroughly as possible to decide what the best investments are for your risk level and never commit yourself to an investment you do not completely understand.

Always Use Your Credit Cards Responsibly. A credit card company is not your friend. Issuing you a large credit limit is giving you enough rope to hang yourself with. Don't get caught in the credit card trap! It is so easy to get in the habit of using your credit card and end up spending more than you can afford. Credit cards are accepted almost everywhere. The convenience, however, is not worth the price you pay if you lose touch with your money. If you use cash for every purchase, aren't you just a little more careful of how you spend your money? Do not become desensitized to the fact that charging is spending *real* money. The green stuff. Treat your credit card like you treat your cash.

If you do use a credit card for convenience, make sure you pay off the balance every month. If you find you spent more than you should have and think you'll carry a balance "just this once," you will be best served by putting the card away until the balance is paid in full. You can easily start carrying a small balance and end up over your head. If you cannot get by without charging, you are living beyond your means and need to fix the situation immediately. Does this sound a bit harsh? Well, few things can ruin your financial life as quickly and as painfully as credit card debt. Clearing your credit card debt can be one of the best investments you can ever make. It is true that you need to establish a credit history. It is also true that a credit card can be invaluable in an emergency. Yet, promise yourself that you will not succumb to the temptation of using credit to purchase the things you really should save up for. Credit cards are best left for emergency use *only*.

Establish a Retirement Account as Early as Possible. I bet you can't believe I'm writing this. Just two chapters ago I was telling you how to get your first job and now I want you to worry about your retirement? Am I kidding? No way! Funding your retirement account now will pay you colossal returns later. Just about any book you pick up on investing for your future will have charts, graphs, and tables explaining how much more you can earn for your retirement by starting sooner rather than later. There's a mega difference.

The best part of saving for your retirement is that the U.S. government wants to help you and has created some incentives for you to save. The IRA (Individual Retirement Account) is one such incentive. An IRA is a personal retirement savings plan that offers you tax advantages. Generally, with a traditional IRA your contribution of earned income may be tax-deductible; taxes are deferred until you are older and you take out the money and the gains. This means that you are setting aside money before you give part of it away in taxes! A Roth IRA is not tax-deductible, but it allows you to put up to a certain amount of earned income away every year, with the benefit of being able to take the money and gains out tax-free in the future.

You decide where you want to set up your IRA, whether it's at a bank, credit union, insurance company or brokerage firm. Make sure you are aware of any fees or loads that may be involved. Setting up an IRA is as easy as opening any other account and the benefit of starting now is tremendous. Make funding your IRA, as fully as you can, a habit you start as soon as possible and continue all your working years.

Your Financial Game Plan

Your Dream

I am financially independent and have all the money I will ever need.

Long-Range Goals

I will purchase a home of my own and do some traveling. I'll continue to make and grow money and to be financially responsible.

Medium-Range Goals

I will continue acquiring the skills I need to have the income that supports the lifestyle I want. Even though I'll have the expense of living on my own, I'll put ten percent of my income into a wealth investment account and learn how to invest to create wealth. I will pay off my student loans and I will fund my retirement account as best I can.

Short-Range Goals

I will have three to six months living expenses saved just in case I ever need the money. I will also have a savings account in place and save enough to cover the expense of moving out on my own. I will find a better job and/or start my own business.

Immediate Action

I'll take advantage of every skill I have and of every opportunity I can create for myself to make more money. Since I'm not yet on my own, I'll faithfully try to put at least 50 percent of my earnings into a savings account. I'll manage my spending so I don't spend more than 50 percent of what I bring home.

Your Present Reality

I'm broke, and I can only work part-time because I'm still in school

If you are employed by a company that offers a 401(k) retirement plan, be sure to study the options carefully so you can take full advantage of the opportunity. A 401(k) is a deferred compensation plan, where you elect to have your employer contribute a portion of your wages to an account set up in your name. With some plans, your employer may match some or all of your contributions. With most plans, you make your own investment decisions, but you are choosing only among investment alternatives offered by the plan, so it is important that you are comfortable with those choices. Although it takes a little time to research and learn about your 401(k) options, it is generally considered a positive move to have such a plan in place and to fund it to the fullest extent that you can or at least enough to take full advantage of your employers matching contribution.

Chart Your Financial Game Plan. Now, I encourage you to take the time to make your financial game plan. Keep in mind the information from the nine positive actions.

Make your plan as detailed or as sketchy as you wish. The details of your plan will change, but your overall commitment to become and remain financially independent should not. The main thing is to have an idea of what you want your financial life to be like and to know some of the steps involved in turning your financial goals into your reality.

There is a great deal involved in maintaining a healthy financial life, but with financial know-how you can and will make the right choices. Make up your mind that you will respectfully manage your money. Trust in your knowledge and in your intuition that you can and will do the right things. Remain motivated for as long as it takes to reach your financial goals and you will give yourself the best chance at having a solid financial future.

Your Checking Account

Once you are receiving regular earnings and are paying your own bills, you are probably going to need to open a checking account. Many employers will only pay employees by direct deposit of wages into an account, so it's time to head for the bank. Or the savings and loan, credit union, or brokerage firm. There have never been so many choices available for handling your money. In today's world, you can bank all over the country without leaving your computer screen. You may end up doing most of your banking and bill paying online. You may want to do all your banking at one location close to where you live. Check out every available option and go with what feels right. Make sure you are happy with the services you get. Unlike the old days when many towns only had one bank, today you have many different options from which to choose.

Once again you are going to have to do some research and leg work. Here are some things to consider when trying to find the checking account that is right for you:

- The best checking account is the one that is totally free. This means there is no fee or service charge to pay every month to maintain the account, no per-check fee, no per-deposit or per-withdrawal fee, no minimum balance required, and no regular charges whatsoever. If you can find it, this is the account for you!

- Keeping in mind that absolutely free is best, the next best checking account is the one with the overall lowest fees and the best services. Find out:

  ✓ What is the monthly service charge? (Don't forget a $10 a month service charge equals $120 every year!)

  ✓ Do you have to maintain a minimum balance?

  ✓ Are there charges involved with getting or using a debit card?

  ✓ Are you charged to use the banks automated teller machine (ATM)?

  ✓ Does the account have **overdraft protection** in the event you bounce a check? Does the overdraft protection involve an additional fee?

  ✓ Are there any other fees you need to be aware of?

- Generally, free accounts do not pay interest. This may work out just fine for you because you won't earn much interest on your checking account funds anyway. Some checking accounts may appear attractive because they pay a low interest rate, but actually involve monthly service fees which are higher than the interest you are likely to earn. Some checking accounts are free if you maintain a minimum balance. Find out how much you will be charged if you ever go under that amount. So much to consider, but you can do it!

- Don't be shy about asking for the services you want if they are not offered to you. Can you have your monthly service fee waived if you direct deposit your paycheck? Want a higher rate of interest on your savings account? Ask the bank manager. A lot of financial institutions are trying to attract students and young people because they are interested in establishing long-term relationships. You may want a checking account right now, but you may need a home loan in the future, and your bank will love the additional business.

- The small bank in your neighborhood may have fewer and smaller fees than the larger one. Be sure to check it out.

- Custom designer checks cost more and may just be an expense you can live without. Consider purchasing your subsequent checks from a discount check company. You may want to check out:

  www.CheckWorks.com

  www.CurrentChecks.com or 800.848.2848

ATM/Debit Card. When you open your checking account, you will probably receive an ATM (automatic teller machine) or **debit** card. An ATM is a terminal that provides you with 24–hour electronic access to your accounts. You can withdraw cash or make a deposit. To use an ATM, you need a personal identification number (PIN) and an ATM or debit card. The same card can be used at many other places as well, such as grocery stores and gas stations.

Using a debit card can be convenient. In fact, you may find that you make most of your purchases with your debit card. Keep these things in mind if you are a debit card user:

- When you make a purchase or withdraw, the money comes out of your account immediately—that instant. The money has to be there. You must keep track of every transaction you make. Write down any account activity right away. This is the trickiest thing about a debit card. Forgetting to write down just one withdrawal from your account could lead to being overdrawn. As with a credit card, don't forget that you are spending real money. If you spend cash, you can tell if it's gone. When you use a debit card, it is not that easy to realize you have spent real money unless you write it down and deduct the amount from your balance.

- ATM charges can add up. If your banks' ATM is free, make it the ATM you use. Using an ATM other than your own bank's can end up costing you plenty in **surcharges.** Want to check your balance before you make a withdrawal? Well then, you may get charged for two transactions! Don't forget that when using your debit card in the grocery store, you can request extra cash. This might save you an ATM fee. Be sure you're using your debit card and not a credit card!

How To Write a Check. Even if you use your debit card for most of your day-to-day transactions and routinely pay your bills online, there might be times when you need to write a check to make a payment from your account. Write clearly and use a black or blue fine line waterproof *permanent* marker or pen.

- Today's date goes on the "Date" line. Putting a future date on a check is called postdating, and very few places will accept a postdated check.

- The correct name of the person or business goes on the "Pay To The Order Of" line. Draw a line over to the dollar sign.

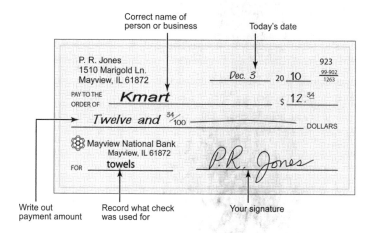

Correct name of person or business — Today's date — Write out payment amount — Record what check was used for — Your signature

- Write out the payment amount on the blank line that leads to the word "Dollars." Use xx/100 for the cents. Draw a line over to the printed word "Dollars." *Example:* Twelve 34/100. Noting the cents and adding a line over to the dollar prevents any additions, such as:

  Twelve hundred———————————DOLLARS.

- Put the amount of the payment, written in digits, by the dollar sign. *Example:* $12.34.

- Your signature goes on the blank line at the bottom right. Make sure you always use the same signature, matching your printed name on the check.

- Never sign your name to a blank check.

- The "Memo" line is for recording for your own purposes what the check is purchasing. For example, "concert tickets" may help refresh your memory of exactly how much your friend owes you for his ticket that you paid for by check.

Watch Out for Bouncing Checks. Bouncing a check can be expensive. This means you wrote a check and your checking account had insufficient funds to pay the amount. A single **returned check** can easily end up costing you over $50 in fees: a charge from your bank for bouncing the check and a charge from the business to which you wrote the check. Being familiar with your financial institution's policy on "*funds available*" will help you avoid this particular mistake.

When you deposit a check (like a personal check from someone else) into your checking account, a portion or the whole amount of the check may not be available for you to use right away. If you do not have other money in the account and you write a check from your account, you may bounce the check you wrote if that check is presented to your bank before the funds you have in the account become available. Trying to guess when a check will get back to your account can be tricky. Some checks are held by whomever you write them to; some checks may clear the same day you write them. It is, of course, best to always have the money available in the account before you write a check. Some funds you deposit into your checking account will be available immediately; some may be available in five days.

Find out if a **hold** is placed on your earnings. If this happens, introduce yourself to the manager and explain that you will be making regular deposits. Chances are very good that you will not have a hold placed on your wages. Be sure you understand your financial institution's policy. Knowing the policy is a good way to avoid those high returned check fees.

Online Banking. Online banking is a fast-growing, fast-evolving banking option. For those who have Internet access, this may be an effective way to pay your bills, add to your savings, and maintain an investment portfolio.

Many banks offer free or low account service charges for automatic bill paying. When checking out your online options, make sure you understand every feature of the service, exactly what the charges are for, and if there are any hidden costs. Will you have to pay an additional charge if you need to pay a bill by phone or mail?

Knowing when a fund transfer takes place is critical to preventing yourself from becoming overdrawn. If you pay your bills online, you need to make sure you know when the bank debits (or takes the money from) your account.

Reminder: In addition to advanced encryption technology and firewall security, your account information online is protected by your personal password. The most difficult passwords to decipher contain both letters and numbers. Make sure yours is not easy to figure out and be sure to guard your password carefully.

Whether you do your banking online or at the local bank, make sure you are comfortable with your banking decision. If you really don't like the choice you made, shop around until you find what you do like. Being uncomfortable with your decision may make handling your finances an unpleasant chore, and may keep you from paying close attention to your money. Try to create a system you enjoy and you will be inclined to stay on top of your finances.

Keeping It Straight. No matter what banking option you choose, you will need to spend a little time keeping things straight and on track. Reconciling your checkbook or balancing your account will help eliminate your chances of becoming overdrawn and is your opportunity to catch a mistake made by your financial institution. Checking these things regularly will head off most serious errors:

- Notice if you have correctly deducted every debit card amount from the money you think you have.
- Check that the written amount of every canceled check is the same amount debited from your account.
- Be sure the check amount is exactly the same amount you entered in your register. For instance, a check may be made out for $13, but you wrote $18 in your register.
- Check your receipts of deposits made during the statement dates to be sure every deposit has been credited

to your account. Make sure you entered every deposit into your register.

- Deduct from your register any service charges that you incurred during the statement period.
- Add any interest payments to your register that were paid during the statement period.
- Notice if you have correctly entered all ATM transactions and fees into your register.

If you receive a paper account statement, keep in mind that your statement only reflects transactions that have taken place during specific dates. If you made a deposit into your account after the statement closing date, it will be noted on next month's statement, so you'll need to *add* the additional deposit to the ending balance noted by your bank. This is your new total. (The flip side of the statement should have a spot for figuring this out—don't use your register.)

Since the checks or debits reflected on your statement are only the amounts that cleared the bank by your monthly closing date — not necessarily all the debits you made or checks that you wrote out —you need to add up those outstanding amounts and *subtract* that amount from your new total. This new amount should be the same as what is in your checkbook register. If it's not, look specifically for the amount that you are off. For example, if you are off by eight dollars and that is the amount of your monthly service charge, you may have forgotten to deduct that charge from your total. Staying on top of your bank statements and not letting them go for too long makes the job a whole lot easier.

Mint.com is a wonderful website designed to help you manage your money and keep track of your spending. Since Mint is a "read-only" service, you can organize and analyze your finances, but you can't actually transfer money in or out of your accounts. It's an easy to use site that offers budgeting tools and other useful financial resources.

Establishing Your Credit Record

It is to your advantage to build a good, solid credit history. Employers sometimes look at a potential employee's **credit report** to determine how responsible they are. Your credit history will be examined when you rent an apartment or apply for an auto or home loan. You need a positive credit history to prove you are a financially responsible person. If you ever mess up—for example, are late with a payment or miss one altogether—it may be reported to one or all of the major credit bureaus. It could take years to get a negative item off your credit report. So it is important not only to establish a credit history, but to keep it unblemished.

- The Credit Card Accountability, Responsibility, and Disclosure (CARD) Act of 2009, requires anyone under 21 to prove a source of income or have a responsible adult cosigner to get a credit card. Any changes to credit limits or other terms on the account must be approved by both the cardholder and the cosigner. The intention here is to help prevent young adults from getting in over their heads with credit card debt.

- You may want to start with a credit card from your favorite clothing store. This could be the easiest card for you to get, but it is also the worst type of card to have if you carry a balance. Only get this type of card if you know you will be paying the total balance due in full and on time. The interest rate could be over twice that of a major credit card company.

- You want the lowest interest rate.

- You do not want to pay an annual fee.

- Know every category of interest charges. For instance, you are charged a higher interest rate on cash advances.

- Make absolutely sure you are credit card savvy. Be happy if you receive a low credit limit and do not be fooled into thinking you "have" the amount of your credit limit. You do not, or you would not be charging. That is just one way credit card debt can sneak up on you and get a stronghold over you. (Again, please remember; if you don't have the real money, don't use the plastic.)

- Be extra careful of "special low introductory rates," "payment holidays," and balance transfers. They are designed to keep your balance as large as possible when your introductory or promotional interest rate expires. Having a large balance on your card when the low rate expires is not a good thing! Your next rate is going to be *significantly* higher. Then you may be tempted to open another credit card account and transfer the old balance. There will be balance transfer fees involved. It can turn into a vicious circle. If you haven't been responsible with one credit card, please do not open another. Not only does having more credit increase your chances of getting in over your head, but having too much credit can sometimes work against you. Often banks are reluctant to give loans to people who have large lines of open credit.

- You may be offered a secured credit card. A secured credit card is one in which you have funds on deposit with the issuer of the card in the amount of your credit limit. This money acts as security in the event you are late with or miss a payment. Before you open a secured credit card account, make sure the issuing company will let you switch to a regular account after a reasonable period of time, usually six months. Also make sure the bank will report your on-time payments to the credit bureaus which will help build your credit rating. If you decide on a secured card, try to find a secured card that does not charge a fee to open the account.

- Be careful not only with your real credit card, but also with the virtual use of your credit card. Do not include the card number in any e-mail message and do not shop from an Internet merchant that does not claim to be on a secure server. Secure websites use encryption software designed to prevent identity theft. Check for a lock icon in your browser's address bar and look for an "s" at the end of "http." in the URL.

Don't be in too much of a rush to get all the credit you can qualify for. Build your credit record slowly. Obtain only one or two credit cards. Find low fixed rates. Stay with a low credit limit, and forget you have the cards.

Paying Your Bills

Most of your bills will be on a monthly cycle. This means your rent, phone, credit card payments, and so forth will all need to be paid every single month. Some billings are every two or three months (such as gas, water, trash, etc.), depending on your situation and location. Then there are the bills that may be due quarterly or semiannually, like insurance premiums. They arrive just about the time you forget all about them. Bills arriving at different times may not be a problem if you always have more than enough money in your accounts to pay them. For those who cut it close every month, balancing the bills can require skill and attention.

- Anticipate not only your monthly bills, but all the bills that will be due in the near future. Don't spend extra money one month because there is no utility bill, only to find you are short when the utility bill does arrive. Plan ahead. Mentally take something out of your checking account every month to cover a bimonthly or quarterly bill. You may even want to subtract the amount from your check register to fool yourself, so you won't spend the money you will be needing.

- Try to pay the bills that are accruing interest as soon as they arrive. Credit card interest is calculated on your average daily balance, so don't let money sit in your checking account while you wait for the statement due date. Pay them as quickly as you can. If you are carrying a credit card balance and have extra

money, make an additional payment any time during
the month.

- For whatever reason, you may be tempted to leave
  your money in your account until the last possible moment before paying your bills. That may be fine, but
  misjudging once and incurring a late charge can be det-
  rimental to your wallet as well as your credit report. Be
  smart about it and make all payments *at least* a week
  before they are due.

- If you have an interest-bearing checking account, you
  may be tempted to leave your money in the account
  until the last possible moment before paying your bills.
  That may be fine if you are good at it, but misjudging
  once and incurring a late charge can eat up more than
  an entire year's worth of interest earnings. Be smart
  about it and mail all payments at least a week before
  they are due.

- Do not pay your bills by mailing cash.

- Don't forget—be good to yourself and pay yourself first!

Loaning Your Money

There's an old saying that goes something like this: "Don't ever
loan anyone more money than you can afford to lose." Chances
are good that you won't get your money back. Only you can decide
if loaning money to someone you know is the right thing to do.
You'll need to consider what the loan will do to your own personal
financial situation. What will the loan do to the relationship you
have with the person who wants the loan? Is it possible the loan
could put a strain on the relationship? Do you feel pressured into
making the loan? Put on the spot? If you decide that you want to
loan someone money (and it's more than just a couple of bucks),
it is reasonable to ask the person to sign a promissory note. You
can get one at most office supply stores. Include the amount borrowed, the amount of the monthly repayment, and the amount
of interest the person will pay for the loan. If your friend refuses
to sign the note and says something like, "You know I'll pay you
back," etc. reconsider loaning the money. Trust your instincts.

There should be a *really* good reason before you ever make a large purchase with your credit card for a friend. Your friend is not being respectful of you if he or she asks you to charge the purchase and tells you, "Don't worry, I'll make the payments." Chances are you *will* end up having to worry about it, every month as you have to track down the payment. Forget it.

It is natural to want to help your family and friends when they need your help. Yet, do it within reason. Like every other decision you make with your money, consider loaning money to anyone very carefully.

Borrowing Money

Owing money to anyone is carrying a burden. Although it may sound like a great idea at a time when you need extra money, borrowing money from relatives and friends can be even more of a burden than having institutional debt, like credit card debt or a bank loan.

Getting a loan from someone you know may change the relationship. A friend may begin to resent you for owing her money, even if it was her idea to loan you the money in the first place!

If you must borrow money from family or friends, make sure you treat the loan the same way you would an institutional loan. Be responsible. Sign a promissory note. Meet or exceed the agreed-upon repayment schedule and get rid of the obligation as soon as possible.

Payday Loan or Advance. Essentially, these businesses operate by giving you cash in advance of your paycheck. Note, that the common cost of borrowing $100 dollars is $15. By calculating this into an annual percentage rate of about 400%, it's easy to see that these loans are not in your best interest. Never get involved with these cash advances unless it is a true emergency and you have absolutely no alternative. Even then, borrow only as much as you can afford to pay with your next paycheck — and still have enough leftover to make it to the following payday.

Using Your Financial Know-How

Because it is so easy to crash and burn on the personal financial obstacle course, many people do. Plenty of adults would love the opportunity to start their financial life over again. While it's not quite possible to go back and have a financial "do over," many people do spend years trying to straighten out the financial mess they've made.

This chapter was designed to prevent you from having a financial blow-out and will help start you on the right course—mainly, not to make a mess of your finances before you really even get going. Cleverer, funnier, and cooler marketing campaigns entice us to spend, spend, and spend some more. Credit card companies try to seduce us, and our economy-driven culture tries to sell us on the erroneous idea that our personal net-worth equates to our personal self-worth. You know better!

Wearing the designer label of the moment may be great if you can afford it, but you are not less of a person if you shop at *Kmart*. As a matter of fact, I know several millionaires who faithfully shop at discount stores and clip coupons, too!

Spending money on yourself and those you love is a wonderful thing, but only if you can afford to do so. Spending more than you should and trying to support a lifestyle you really can't afford are the quickest ways to fall into financial trouble.

How do you know how to make the right moves with your money? Gain financial knowledge and practice putting that knowledge to work in your everyday life. Read everything you can about money management and the energy of money. Go to the library and read the monthly money magazines. Ask for advice from the people in your life who appear to be managing their money successfully. You may be surprised at what you hear. You will benefit by hearing the mistakes others have made and from learning the strategies that others have found helpful.

Many interesting Internet sites offer useful information to help you manage your money. You may want to start with these:

Alliance Credit Counseling: *www.knowdebt.org*
This non-profit service organization offers easy-to-understand information on many money management skills.

America Saves: *www.americasaves.org*
    Useful information on saving money and building personal wealth.

Bankrate, Inc.: *www.bankrate.com*
    Free financial rate information, advice and tools.

Choose to Save Education Program: *www.choosetosave.org*

Federal Reserve–Personal Financial Education: *www.federalreserveeducation.org*

Mutual Fund Investor's Center: *www.mfea.com*
    Information from the Mutual Fund Education Alliance.

National Endowment for Financial Education: *www.nefe.org* or 303.741.6333.

Roth IRA information: *www.rothira.com*
    Current information on the Roth IRA.

Smart About Money: *www.smartaboutmoney.org*
    Offers information on a broad range of financial topics to help you make positive financial decisions and to reach your financial goals.

360 Degrees of Financial Literacy: *www.360financialliteracy.org* and *www.feedthepig.org*
    This volunteer effort of the nation's Certified Public Accountants offers some of the best resources and tools to help understand and manage your personal finances through every stage of life.

U.S. Financial Literacy and Education Commission: *www.mymoney.gov*

U.S. Citizens for Fair Credit Card Terms, Inc.: *www.CardRatings.com*. Credit card rating information

Women's Institute for Financial Education: *www.wife.org* or 760.736.1660.

Hint: There are several popular software programs available to help you handle your money, including the current edition of Quicken.

Related Resources

Dave Ramsey's Complete Guide to Money: The Handbook of Financial Peace University by Dave Ramsey. Lampo Press; 2012.

The Difference: How Anyone Can Prosper in Even The Toughest Times by Jean Chatzky. Crown Business; 2010.

Make Money, Not Excuses: Wake Up, Take Charge, and Overcome Your Financial Fears Forever by Jean Chatzky. Crown Business; 2008.

The Money Book for the Young, Fabulous and Broke by Suze Orman. Riverhead Trade; 2007.

The Money Class: How to Stand in Your Truth and Create the Future You Deserve by Suze Orman. Spiegel & Grau; 2012.

Personal Finance For Dummies by Eric Tyson. Check for the current edition.

Please Send Money: A Financial Survival Guide for Young Adults on Their Own by Dara Duguay. Sourcebooks, Inc.; 2008.

Put More Cash in Your Pocket: Turn What You Know into Dough by Loral Langemeier. Harper Paperbacks; 2009.

The Richest Man in Babylon by George S. Clason.

Rule #1: The Simple Strategy for Successful Investing in Only 15 Minutes a Week! by Phil Town. Three Rivers Press; 2007.

Seven Strategies for Wealth & Happiness: Power Ideas from America's Foremost Business Philosopher by Jim Rohn.

Start Young, Finish Rich by David Bach. Doubleday Canada; 2009.

Your Money, Day One: How to Start Right and End Rich by Michael J. Wagner. BookSurge Publishing; 2009.

> *"No matter who you are, making informed decisions about what you do with your money will help build a more stable financial future for you and your family."*
> *Alan Greenspan*

Chapter 4

Setting Up Your Home

What You Need

You can eventually live a very sucessful life even if you start out with nothing more than the clothes on your back. It's been done. Yet, I hope you start out living on your own by being as prepared as possible. As you plan ahead, take into consideration all the wordly goods that are involved with setting up a home. Fortunately, if we have to, we can get along just fine without most of the stuff. There are things that you need and things that would be nice to have. You don't have to come up with everything at once.

The Basics:

- Mattress
- Set of sheets
- Blanket
- Pillow
- Towels
- Frying pan

- Sauce pan
- Can opener
- Large mixing spoon
- Plate, bowl, glass, and mug
- Knife, fork, and spoon
- Lamp

Looking at the previous short list, you can see that if survival depended on it, we really could get by without most of the items. The same goes for the following expanded list of the things that would be great to have when you move into your own place. Don't worry if you don't have everything. You will eventually. Acquiring items can be something that you do over an extended period of time. Use the checklist here as a basic guide to making your own list of things you need.

Try to Acquire:

- Baking dish (9 x 13)
- Bath towels
- Beach towel
- Bed frame
- Bed pillows
- Blanket
- Box springs
- Bucket
- Can opener
- Clock
- Coffeemaker
- Cookie sheet
- Dishes, set
- Drinking glasses
- Flatware
- Sofa
- Spatula
- Table and chairs
- Tablecloth or placemats

- Hand towels
- Kitchen knives
- Kitchen towels
- Mattress
- Mattress cover
- Measuring cups
- Measuring spoons
- Mixer
- Mixing bowls
- Mixing spoon
- Muffin pan
- Pot holders
- Pots and pans
- Salt and pepper shakers
- Sheets, set
- Toaster
- Vacuum
- Vegetable peeler
- Washcloths

When your family and friends ask, "What do you want for your birthday?", you know what the answer is. Letting the word out that you will soon be living on your own may bring household donations that you could really use. You can also find items that have plenty of use still in them at garage sales and thrift stores. Consider bartering as well as shopping at clearance and close-out sales.

Tools. In addition to household items, I recommend you start collecting the basic tools you will need for your tool kit:

Minimum Tool List
- Hammer and assorted nails
- Pliers
- Scissors
- Screwdrivers—Phillips and flat-head, and assorted screws
- Utility knife—with reversable, retractable blade

Expanded Tool List
- Duct tape
- Hammer and assorted nails
- Industrial-strength glue
- Pliers
- Plunger
- Scissors
- Screwdrivers—cordless power screwdrivers are great!
- Staple gun
- Tape measure
- Utility knife—with reversable, retractable blade
- Wrench—adjustable

Where Will You Live?

The highlight of moving out on your own is the actual moving into your own place. You've planned, worked, and thought about it for such a long time, and the day finally arrives when you are ready to start hunting for your new home.

The city you choose to live in will most likely be dictated by your job, school, or family connections. The actual address you decide to call home will most likely be chosen on the basis of what you can afford. We all want to live in as safe and as comfortable a place as our finances will allow. The first experience most of us have living on our own is not with home ownership, but with renting. So how do you know how much rent you can reasonably pay each month?

When you set about renting a unit, you must supply the owner or manager with some of your personal information. The rental application will ask your income. Your verifiable income (that which can be proven, such as from your employer) should be at least three or four times the rent you are considering. This means you probably won't be able to qualify for the unit if more than 25 percent to 33 percent of your monthly income is to be used for your rent. For example, if you bring home $2,400 a month, you shouldn't consider spending more than $800 a month for housing.

> Your verifiable income (that which can be proven, such as from your employer) should be at least three or four times the rent you are considering.

This rule is not etched in stone. You may find a landlord who doesn't care how much you make as long as you pay the rent in full and on time. Perhaps you know you can easily go without spending money in one area, such as on entertainment, if it means you can afford to live where you really want. Take your personal spending habits into consideration and arrange your priorities, keeping the 33 percent rule in mind. Once you figure out how much you can afford, don't be tempted to spend "just a little bit more." The amount of $830 sounds pretty close to $800, but reaching for that extra $30 every month might turn into too much of a stretch. Remember, starting and keeping your monthly rent payment as low as possible will be to your advantage.

It's not uncommon for a young person to have some help with the first rental experience. Perhaps if you cannot qualify for a rental unit due to lack of a credit history, for instance—a parent or other family member may be willing to cosign or be responsible with you. That person includes his or her financial and credit information in the application and enters into the agreement, even though he or she will not be living with you. If you get a cosigner, make sure you treat the agreement responsibly.

Take extra pains to pay the rent on time and in full. Someone has stepped out on a limb for you and you need to show that person that his or her trust and efforts were not misplaced.

Before Your Search Begins. After you have decided the maximum monthly payment you can afford, it's time to prepare for the search. Before you begin looking at rental units, take the following steps to ensure your search goes smoothly:

1. If you have a credit history, get a copy of your credit report. This ensures that you are aware of its contents. You do not want to be caught off-guard if there's a negative item in the report. If the report contains a mistake, do what you can to correct it, by contacting each of the three main credit reporting companies. You can order one free credit report from each of the three companies every year. To do so, visit the official central site *www.annualcreditreport.com*. Bypass other places that offer "free" reports and go directly to this source.

Equifax :	800.685.1111	*www.equifax.com*
Experian:	888.397.3742	*www.experian.com*
Trans Union:	800.916.8800	*www.transunion.com*

2. Obtain permission from two or three people to use their names and telephone numbers as possible references.

3. In addition to references, have other information ready that will be requested, such as:

   ✓ The name, address and phone number of your employer

   ✓ Current pay stub

   ✓ Previous employment information

   ✓ Social Security and driver's license numbers

4. Decide what you are looking for. What factors are the most important? How much room do you need? Do you need a place that allows pets? Do you want the respon-

sibility of a yard? Having an idea of what your requirements are will help you focus your search.

5. Check a street map of your town. Are some neighbor-
hoods more convenient for your situation than others?
Do you have favorite areas where you would like to
live? For instance, finding a place that is close to your
job or university may be important to you.

6. Make a list of the available rentals which meet your
needs. Today, even with online searches, often the best
resource is still your local newspaper, especially the
weekend real estate section. You can also obtain rental
guides. They can be found at grocery stores, gas stations, colleges, real estate offices, and so on.

You may want to look into professionally run properties,
such as those offered by a property management company or
real estate office. Rental agents are paid their fee by the property
owner, so you do not directly pay for the assistance. Professional
property managers are typically very much aware not only of
owners' rights and responsibilities, but of the rights of tenants
as well. Not all real estate offices handle rentals, but you may
want to try to find one in your area that does.

What to Look For. In choosing the place that is right for you,
knowing what to look out for is as important as knowing what to
look for. Try to give yourself as much time as possible to make the
decision that is right for you. Don't be in such a hurry to move
in that you overlook something important, such as realizing after
it's too late that you've moved into a building in which neighbors
start to party just about the time you need to get to sleep. You
cannot be passive in your search. You have to take the lead and
ask the right questions. Here are a few suggestions:

- Pay close attention to the neighborhood. Is it well
tended? Do you feel safe? How far is it from your work,
university, place of worship, and so forth?

- Try to visit the unit in the daytime. This allows you to
notice how much natural light the unit gets and helps

in identifying what kind of shape it's in. You can see dirt, marks, and stains, better in daylight.

- If a unit becomes a real possibility, try to revisit it at night. Look at the neighborhood again. Look at the exterior lighting. Notice the lighting in pathways, alleys, hallways, and stairwells. Does the surrounding environment appear to be a safe one?

- Once you think you have found the place that is right for you, don't be shy about meeting your prospective neighbors. Ask them about their experiences with the building's management and if they would recommend a move into the building. Ask about their experiences getting repairs taken care of. Ask about noise. Ask about bugs. Are the neighbors being friendly? You may find out more than you expected.

- Take notes while you are searching. After looking at many different units for several days or weeks, it is easy to get confused. When you find the unit that is the one for you, and you think you are ready to commit, take detailed notes about the entire condition of the unit and what has been discussed with the owner or manager. For instance, if the carpet is stained, write a detailed description of the condition and have the landlord or manager sign the documentation. This acknowledgement may help prevent any disputes over responsibility when you move out. You can also take photos or make a video before you bring in your belongings. This will show the exact condition of the unit when you moved in.

- Always look at the exact unit that you will be living in, not one similar to it, such as a model. Never sign a lease for a unit sight unseen. Never.

- Find out if any utilities are included with the rent. For instance, the water bill is often paid by the owner and not the separate tenants. You may want to ask what the average utility bills cost for heating and/or cooling to determine if your budget allows for this expense.

If your first impression of the unit is positive, look a little deeper. Make sure everything works as it should. Don't be shy. Ask questions and run some tests:

- Does the shower have enough water pressure?
- Run the water in all the faucets; check the pressure and determine if the water is hot.
- Flush the toilet.
- Open and close the windows; do they stick? Lock securely?
- Do all the doors close as they should?
- Try the locks. Find out if they have been changed or rekeyed since the last tenant. Ask if you can have this done.
- Look for leaks and water damage on the ceilings and floors. Look under the sinks.
- Do you smell mold or mildew?
- Does the thermostat work properly? Heater? Air-conditioner?
- Do the walls have holes, dents, marks, or cracks?
- Do all the kitchen appliances work?
- Are there smoke detectors in working order in the unit?
- Where will you park your car?
- What do the common areas look like? Are they clean and maintained? What kind of shape is the laundry room in?
- If there are shared facilities, such as a pool, what are the hours of operation?
- Is the prospective landlord or property manager friendly and responsive to your questions?
- Does he or she appear to be someone whom you will be comfortable entering into a contract with?

- Make sure your questions and concerns are stated directly and to the point. It is considered misrepresentation if an owner or manager lies to you, but it is your responsibility to ask the questions that may be of importance. For instance, you should ask, "Has the carpeting been professionally cleaned since the last tenant moved out?" instead of asking, "Is the carpet clean?"
- Find out the policy regarding your pet before you get too involved. Pets are forbidden from some units entirely. Some rentals allow pets only if an additional security deposit is paid. Check first.
- Is the asking rent in line with comparable units?

Your Rental Agreement

Great! You have finally found the place you want to call home. It suits both your needs and your wants. You have checked absolutely everything for potential problems. You are ready to pay the rent and pick up the key. Right? Well, almost.

The last big consideration here is your rental agreement or lease. You need to read, agree, and honor it completely. It's a contract. It spells out what the obligations are for both you and your landlord. It is in your best interest to make sure you thoroughly understand the document.

The time to request changes to a rental document is before you sign it and assume responsibility for its terms. As you read the lease or rental agreement, take note of any modifications you wish to make. If the landlord agrees to your requests, make sure the necessary changes are made on the document and that the landlord initials each change and signs and dates the modified version in ink. Make sure you get a copy.

If you accept the terms of the document, but only if certain conditions are met by the landlord, such as the unit must be painted first, make sure you get the exact conditions in writing, with a date and the signature of the landlord or manager.

Make sure you are clear about what will occur if you breach or break the document. For instance, if you sign a 12-month lease, but your employer transfers you to another state after 7-months, what will be your financial obligation to your landlord? Can you **sublease** the unit?

Take your time and read the document carefully. All rental documents are not the same. Ask questions and refuse to be rushed into signing. Make sure you understand the terms regarding the following:

The Monthly Rent. You are obligating yourself to pay the agreed-upon amount of rent for the agreed-upon amount of time. Find out exactly how your payments are to be made. For instance, where is the payment to be mailed? What day is it due? Are there additional fees involved if you are late? By how many days?

Term of the Tenancy. The length of time you and the landlord agree to be obligated to the rental document is called "the term of tenancy." A rental document is either a fixed-term lease or a rental agreement. Rental agreements may run for several months or run month-to-month and self-renew unless terminated by either party. Leases are usually for one year. When the lease expires, either party can decline to renew it, or it continues on a month-to-month basis.

Security Deposit and Other Fees. In addition to the rent, you will almost always need to make a **security deposit.** This is money that will be held by the landlord to offset any damages made to the property while you are living there. Make sure you understand the conditions for getting your deposit back when you eventually move out. This is why documenting the condition of the unit before you move in is important. Is any portion of your security deposit nonrefundable? Will a cleaning charge be deducted from your deposit when you vacate the unit? How and *when* will your deposit be returned? There may be other fees involved with your lease. Are you required to make an additional deposit for your pet?

Repairs and Maintenance. You will be required to keep your unit clean and sanitary and will be held responsibile if you damage the property by abuse or neglect. It is your responsibility to inform the landlord of any defective and dangerous conditions to the property. It is the landlord's responsibility to keep the premises in livable condition. As you can imagine, this can be subject to interpretation. The landlord is not legally responsible for strictly cosmetic-type repairs. Of course you can request the yellowing wallpaper be replaced and of course the request may be denied. Find out what kind of repairs or alterations you are allowed to do yourself. Most property owners understand the importance of keeping their property in good shape and appreciate being alerted to a potentially serious problem. Make sure your rental document outlines how repairs will be addressed.

Special Rules or Restrictions. Being well-informed on the rules and restrictions relating to your unit can save a lot of misunderstandings. If you are renting a condo, the rules are called the CCRs. These codes, covenants, and restrictions spell out very clearly what is acceptable and what is not. The same may apply to the terms of your rental document. There may be a clause relating to disruptive behavior. There may be a restriction on the lengh of time a houseguest can stay with you. Understand the restrictions before you agree to adhere to them.

Vacating the Property. What does the rental document require of you when it's time to move on? How much notice do you need to give? Will you be required to allow the unit to be shown to prospective tenants when you are not present? When you move out, you may want to do a "walk through" with the landlord and also document the condition of the unit by photographs or video to make sure no misunderstandings arise regarding the condition of the property.

When you sign a lease or rental agreement, you are entering into a legal contract, but the agreement itself must be legal. This means that it must comply with all relevant laws. Laws and ordinances exist to protect both the property owner's and the tenant's rights. Learn what your rights are with regard to your landlord entering your unit. This can be a flashpoint if both parties are not aware of the law. A good rental document is thorough and clearly outlines the responsiblities of all persons involved.

A good rental document is fair to all parties. For instance, you should probably avoid signing a rental contract that states you "agree to pay all costs for court proceedings brought forth by either party." Use your common sense and get everything spelled out as clearly as possible, right down to the use of nails for hanging pictures.

Do not hesitate to try to negotiate the terms of your rental document. It is better than trying to live with conditions you find objectionable.

Roommates

Often, the only way it's financially possible to move away from home and live on your own is to live with a roommate, or perhaps several. This does not necessarily mean that you are not making it on your own. You still must be responsible and meet all your obligations, but sharing expenses may make the dream of being independent financially possible.

Of course, you must choose your roommate carefully, although going off to college often means having to experience the challenge of arbitrary roommate assignment. Yet, whether you know your roommate ahead of time or meet them on check-in day, being prepared for the experience may go a long way to contributing to a successful situation. While it helps if you and your roommate both like the same lifestyle, even the oddest matched couple can survive together if they thoughtfully make and honor a mutual agreement. Yes, this does mean another written agreement. Having a written agreement to pull out when sticky situations arise can be in both your best interests.

There will be differences. Differences between people who live together are a way of life. Yet the differences do not have to be a problem. Having an agreement worked out ahead of time will help head off issues before they become big problems. Work on the agreement together, keeping equality in mind.

Are both of your names on the lease? One person being responsible for the terms of the lease and the other being able to walk away at any time may not be the best arrangement. How are you going to split utilities? Consider a policy on all aspects of living together, such as the cleaning, mutual expenses, guests, food, and even quiet time. Keep in mind you must always honor the agreement and that it isn't necessary to like someone to get along with them.

Utilities

You've signed your lease, paid your rent and security deposit, and just picked up the key to your new place. The next step is getting the utilities turned on and in your name.

Your new landlord, manager, or agent probably has the names and numbers of the utility companies that service your area. You may even be able to transfer services from the previous tenants and avoid full set-up charges. Be sure to ask. The utility companies are listed in your local phone book, or of course you can ask your new neighbors for the names of the companies.

When you call to set up your new accounts, make sure you have your personal information handy, including:

- Your driver's license number or other identification information
- Your Social Security number
- The exact address of your new place
- The day you want the services to start
- Your employment information, including the company's name, address, phone number, and the date you started working there
- Your bank information, including a credit card number if you have one

Depending on your credit history or the utility company's policy, you may be required to submit a deposit for the services. This will usually be returned to you after a certain amount of time, usually one year.

Since some utilities require more time than others to get setup, make the necessary arangements as soon as possible after your rental agreement is finalized.

Water and Sewer. If your rental unit does not include the water and sewer, you will need to contact the Water Department.

Gas and Electric. These utilities are often combined or may require separate accounts. Generally your account can be set up in a day.

Phone and Cable. Depending on your area, these services may take several days or over a week to get in place. Be careful not to sign-up for more services than you really need.

Garbage. Depending on where you live, you may need to set up an account with the Sanitation Department.

Reminder: If you are sharing expenses with a roommate, consider very carefully the arrangement regarding the responsibility of the utilities. Will the bill be in both your names? If so, your roomate will also need to provide the necessary application information to the service providers.

Moving

No matter how simple or involved your move may be, keep the following in mind:

Be prepared. Do whatever you can do ahead of time. If your new place requires any attention, such as a cleaning or some shelf paper, now is the time to get it done. It will be much easier facing it now than waiting until after you've moved in.

- Fill out a mail forwarding card from the post office. Be sure to include the date you want the forwarding to begin.

- Notify everyone of your new address and phone number.

- If you are moving out of town, wrap up any unfinished business. For example, did you get your dirty clothes out of your locker at the gym? Return your library books? Return everything you've borrowed from friends? Pick up your dry cleaning? Visit or call your family and friends?

- If your pet is going with you and will need a new license or tag, make sure you have it's imunization certificate.

- If you are not using a moving company, make sure you have plenty of help. You may want to line up more help than you need just in case someone doesn't show.

- If you are renting or borrowing a truck, make sure it is one you can drive. Don't get stuck with a stick shift if you can only drive an automatic.

- Do you need to rent or borrow a dolly? This can make a huge difference if you are moving large, heavy items.

- Think about where you are going to place your furniture. Even good friends run out of patience picking up and putting down a couch a dozen times.

- If you are planning to use a professional moving service, do some research to make sure you are dealing with a reputable company. Stay away from a company that gives you a quote over the phone or Internet without actually looking at your stuff, or from a company that wants cash or a very large deposit before the move. Obtain at least three legitimate estimates before you decide which company to use. The estimates will either be binding (you will not be charged more than the estimated amount) or nonbinding (there is no guarantee that the final cost will be as low or as high as the estimate.) Here again, you will be entering into a written agreement so make sure you are aware and understand all the details. It is important not only to finalize the pick-up date and time, but to make sure you will have your things delivered exactly when you need them. Get it in writing.

Gather some things together to have available on moving day:

Moving Supplies
- Can opener
- Carton sealing tape
- Cleaning products and cleaning cloths
- Dish soap
- First aid kit that contains a pain reliever
- Hand soap
- Light bulbs
- Paper cups for water or drinks
- Paper towels
- Snacks
- Toilet paper
- Tools: utility knife, hammer, screwdrivers, and pliers
- Towels for the bathroom and kitchen
- Trash bags

Moving Out. If you use any boxes that are not new, such as from the grocery store or a friend's garage, check each one for insects and insect eggs. You don't want to inadvertently *bring* cockroaches, or other insects into your new place.

Even if you are only moving down the street, you'll need to pack carefully.

- Keep in mind the heavier the item is, the smaller its box should be.

- Heavy items go in the bottom of the box with smaller, lighter items on top.
- Try to use unprinted newsprint instead of old newspapers to wrap items. Newspaper ink will rub off.
- Prevent items from shifting in their box by crumpling up the wrapping paper to fill all empty spaces. You can also use towels or clothes for this, but it makes unpacking more complicated.
- Think about unpacking when you pack. Items that go together should be in the same box. Packing by room will make unpacking easier.
- Clearly label your boxes—bedroom, kitchen, and so on.
- When loading the trailer or truck, be sure to put the heaveist things in first and keep them the lowest.
- Carefully keep track of your valuables, important papers, and medications. Keep them with you.

Moving In

- Turn on the refrigerator.
- If you have not already done so, take time out on moving day to familiarize yourself with the electric circuit breaker or fuse box. Find the location of your gas and water main valves. Learn how to shut them off in an emergency situation.
- Put the boxes in the room they are labeled to go in. Keeping all the boxes together in the dining room, for example, and unpacking them one at a time may be neater, but may also involve more time and effort.
- Prioritize your unpacking and setting up. For instance, set up and make your bed before you get too tired. If you have to go to work the next day, make sure you can find your clothes.

- Once everything is moved in, take your time unpacking. If any item is dirty, now is the time to clean it. Consider very carefully the best way to set up your new home.

Reminder: If you have permanently changed states, you will need to get a new driver's license and change your vehicle registration. Also contact the Board of Elections if you wish to register to vote.

Organization

Chances are you will organize your own place similiarly to the home you grew up and were comfortable in. The point here, though, is to actually do some thoughtful organization. Being well-organized will not only save you valuable time, but will save you unnecessary stress as well. Who wants to run around hunting for car keys when late for a movie? Yet, the forces of natural law are working against you here. Are you familar with **entropy**? If you don't work to keep your place clean, it's going to turn into a mess. Order goes to chaos. It's a fact of life. The quip we are all familiar with—"a place for everything and everything in its place"—has been around forever with good reason. It's the key to maintaining order. Here are a few tips you may want to consider:

- Remember your cubby from day care or kindergarten? It was your personal little area to put your own stuff and you knew right where everything went. Having such an area in your own place can be a great time-saver. Faithfully put your outgoing mail there, and you will automatically grab it on your way out. The same goes for library books that need to be returned, outgoing dry cleaning, the gift you need to deliver, and anything else you need to have with you when you run errands.

- Choose a convenient, safe, *private* place to keep your keys, purse, or wallet.

- Organize to fit your lifestyle. Are you more inclined to come in the door and toss your jacket somewhere than to walk to the closet and hang it up? If you are, you may want to install a wall coatrack. Do you need to set up a special area to do paperwork or will anywhere do just fine? Think about what will work the best for your individual needs.

- Whether it's clothes, bedding, or kitchenware, items that are used together should be kept together.

- Items should be kept closest to where they are going to be used the most.

- The most frequently used items belong in the most accessible spots.

- Think ahead and organize to make getting out of the house in the morning as easy as possible.

- Put cleaning supplies in the area where you use them, not together in a closet somewhere, unless they are in a caddy or basket with a handle that you can carry with you from room to room.

- If you have a land line, arrange the area by the phone to include:

  ✓ List of emergency numbers, including those of a neighbor, your doctor, poison control center, and your landlord.

  ✓ List of frequently called numbers, like your favorite take-out restaurant.

  ✓ Pens and paper

  ✓ Calendar (Fill in all the birthdays you need to remember for the year when you put the calendar up.)

- Invest in a good quality flashlight and keep it close to your bed.

- Establish and maintain a simple, logical filing system:

  Basic File Headings
  - ✓ Automobile
  - ✓ Bills That Need To Be Paid*
  - ✓ Checking Account Statements
  - ✓ Credit Card Information (account numbers and customer service numbers)
  - ✓ Insurance
  - ✓ Medical
  - ✓ Paid Bills (statement stubs and receipts)
  - ✓ Tax Documents
  - ✓ Warranties and Manuals

- What's in your wallet? Take a few minutes and make a detailed list of the important things you have in your wallet or purse, in case you lose it or it's stolen. File the list. Carry:

  - ✓ ATM card
  - ✓ Cash, not more than for one week
  - ✓ Credit card, only one
  - ✓ Driver's license or photo identification card
  - ✓ Make an *In Case of Emergency* card that lists the names and numbers of who should be called, your next of kin and important medical information a first responder would need to know.
  - ✓ Emergency money – try to keep at least $20 tucked away
  - ✓ Medical/prescription insurance card
  - ✓ Supermarket discount card

---

*If you create a "Bills That Need To Be Paid" file, make sure you check it regularly. Otherwise, use a container to keep the bills organized and in sight so you will not forget about them.

- Make sure you do not carry around your Social Security card or anything else you don't really need to have with you.
- Process your mail every day. You may want to do this standing by the trash can.
- If you are going to recycle, set up a system that makes it easy for you to faithfully keep at it. Even if you think it is too much for you to think about now, perhaps you can at least commit to recycling glass and cans.
- Most importantly, deal with things as you go along. If you bring home dry cleaning, take the time to walk it to the closet. Clean the kitchen after you eat, not three days later.

Experiment until you find the organizational solutions that work for you. But remember, even the best organization ends up being useless if you don't work at maintaining the order.

> Check out *www.Earth911.com* "for all you need to know about reducing your impact, reusing what you've got and recycling your trash."

Supplies

Shopping List—Nonfood Items

- Aluminum foil
- Cellophane tape
- Coffee filters (if you make coffee)
- Dishwasher detergent (if you have a dishwasher)
- Dishwashing detergent
- Facial tissue
- Garbage bags
- Light bulbs
- Matches

- Muffin pan liners
- Paper napkins
- Paper towels
- Plastic food storage bags
- Plastic wrap
- Soap
- Steel wool soap pads or sponges
- Toilet paper
- Waxed paper

Additional Items You May Need

- All purpose stain remover
- Batteries
- Chlorine bleach
- Cleanser
- Fabric softener
- Glass cleaner
- Laundry detergent
- Leather cleaner and conditioner (for shoes)
- Liquid detergent for fine fabrics
- Multipurpose cleaner
- Oxygen bleach
- Shoe polish

Medications and Emergency Supplies. Having basic over-the-counter medications or natural remedies, as well as emergency supplies around the house is part of setting up your new place. Use the following lists to help you prepare the essentials that you should always have on hand. Decide whether you want to combine your medications with your first aid supplies. Either way, store all the supplies in an easily acessible, easily transportable container. In the event of an emergency, you will want to have them with you.

Medications

- Antacid (such as Mylanta)
- Antidiarrhea medication (such as Imodium A-D)
- Antihistamine (such as Benadryl, for allergic reactions)
- Cough syrup
- Decongestant
- Pain reliever (aspirin or nonaspirin)
- Throat lozenges
- Good thermometer

Note these important tips:

- Read all labels and accompanying information carefully and take only as directed.
- Keep all medications in their original containers, and toss them after the expiration date. (Be sure to take the full dosage of prescribed antibiotics.)
- Store your medications in a cool, dark, and dry place.
- Keep up-to-date with your prescription medications. Plan ahead to get your refill *before* you run out.

Call The Poison Control Center at 800.222.1222 if you have a poisoning emergency.

First Aid Supplies. Keep your first aid supplies in an easily accessible place (preferably the kitchen where accidents are likely to occur.) Store the supplies in a container with a handle to make it easy to grab on the go. Be sure to return or replace items after use.

Household First Aid Supplies

- Adhesive bandages (assorted sizes)
- Adhesive tape
- Antibiotic ointment
- Antiseptic (such as rubbing alcohol)

- Calamine lotion
- Cleansing agent or soap
- Elastic bandage
- Hydrogen peroxide
- Latex gloves
- Roller bandages
- Safety pins (large and small)
- Scissors
- 2 small bath towels
- Sterile cotton
- Sterile dressings (assorted sizes)
- Sterile roll of gauze
- Tweezers (to remove splinters and glass)
- Wooden tongue blades (for finger splints)

Emergency Supplies. While natural disasters may be more likely in some geographic areas than others, you should be prepared for an emergency situation no matter where you live. Many emergencies, such as a hazardous material evacuation, can happen anywhere. We may never know when a disaster will strike, but we can take comfort in knowing we are prepared. The following information is a short excerpt from "Disaster Supplies Kit" developed by the Federal Emergency Management Agency (FEMA) and the American Red Cross. Call your local Red Cross chapter for geographically specific, natural disaster preparedness information. For instance, if you live in southern California you should keep an earthquake survival kit in your car as well as in your home. Keep your supplies in a lightweight container that is easy to carry if you have to evacuate.

- Store at least a three-day supply of nonperishable food. Include ready-to-eat canned meats, fruits, vegetables, and juices. Also include high energy foods, such as granola and snack bars, trail mix and peanut butter.
- You need at least one gallon of water per person per day. Have at least three gallons.

- One complete change of clothes, including a pair of sturdy shoes.
- Blanket or sleeping bag
- Flashlight (with extra batteries)
- Battery-operated radio (with extra batteries)
- Can opener (nonelectric – or pack only pop top canned food in your kit)
- Multipurpose tool
- Cash and change
- Personal documents; copies of important papers such as deed/lease to home, passports, birth certificates, insurance policies and proof of address.
- Family and emergency contact information
- Paper cups and plates, plastic utensils
- Matches in a waterproof container
- Toilet paper, moist towelettes, garbage bags and plastic ties for personal sanitation
- Soap and personal hygiene items
- Medications (7 day supply), medication list and pertinent medical information

Contact the American Red Cross at *www.redcross.org* or *800.733.2767* for assistance or additional information. You can support the Red Cross by buying emergency preparedness kits and supplies from them directly.

Consider using a password protected USB device to store your important electronic files, including your financial account numbers and the customer service numbers of the institutions you use. Having everything organized and easily accessible after a disaster may help you get up and running faster. Eventually, you might want to consider researching and using a cloud storage service provider.

Additional Resources

- Visit Operation HOPE at *www.operationhope.org* to download and print the document *Emergency Financial First Aid Kit*. This simple tool is designed to help you have your most important financial information in order and on hand in the event of an emergency.

- The Department of Homeland Security's *Ready Campaign* encourages individuals to prepare themselves for the unexpected. Their web site, *www.ready.gov*, is a great source of information, tools and checklists.

- If there is a presidentially declared disaster in your area, The Federal Emergency Management Agency, (FEMA) may be able to provide you with assistance. The Disaster Assistance number is *800.621.3362* and the web address is *www.fema.gov*. *Are You Ready?* is an in-depth FEMA guide to citizen disaster preparedness that you can download from the web site or order by calling *800.480.2520*.

Safety and Security

Fire Safety. Few people realize how fast a fire can take hold and how quickly it can become uncontrollable. Please take the danger of fire seriously.

- Make sure you have at least one smoke alarm and that it has good batteries. Many people use New Year's Day as a reminder to change the batteries in their smoke detectors.

- Buy one or several multipurpose fire extinguishers. At a minimum, keep one handy in the kitchen and know how to use it.

- Keep baking soda or flour by the stove. Have it at arm's reach, and if something on the stove starts to burn, you can quickly douse the flames.

- Be careful not to set your pot holders on fire.

- Electrical outlets should not be overloaded.

Burning candles is once again very popular. Use extra caution here. Don't use lighted candles in windows or near exits.

The National Fire Protection Association offers tips regarding candles. The following is taken from their recommendations:

- Make sure the candle is in a sturdy holder that will not tip over.

- Place the candle on a sturdy piece of furniture in the center of a one-foot "circle of safety." This means you have checked and there is absolutely nothing within at least a one-foot radius that can possibly ignite, such as wallpaper, curtains or draperies, towels, shelves, plants, and silk flowers.

- Absolutely *never* leave the room or fall asleep with a candle burning.

- Stop burning your candle when it gets down to half an inch from the base. Throw it away.

- Blow out candles or use a snuffer, but never use water to extinguish the flame. Water can cause wax to splatter and can spread the flames.

Personal Precautions. Take a class in self-defense. Please don't put it off. You will feel more confident and secure knowing you know the basics of protecting yourself. Check for classes at your local YMCA, community, or adult education center.

- Do not label your keys with your name or address. Give an extra set of keys to a relative if you wish, but do not label them correctly. Doing so may allow someone to enter your home if the keys are lost or stolen. Carry a spare car key or key card in your wallet.

- Always have your door key ready before you approach your home.

- Always pay close attention to what is happening around you.

- Buy a small flashlight that hooks onto your key ring. This is a big help in locating a keyhole in the dark.

- Set an interior light or radio on a timer when you are away at night.

- Make sure you look in the rearview mirror and close your automatic garage door (if you have one) as soon as your car clears the door.

- Make sure your garage door opener is always in the same place. You should not be sitting in your car scrounging around for the opener. You may choose not to leave the opener in your car when you park outside your garage.

- Take your parking ticket with you when you park in a pay lot.

- If you leave your car somewhere overnight, remove all identifying information. You don't want to return to find your car stolen *and* your home broken into.

- When driving, never let yourself get caught between two cars. Carjackers often work in pairs.

- Don't ever pull off the road when driving by yourself at night, except in a true emergency.

- If you believe you have been intentionally rammed from the rear, proceed to a populated, well-lit area or a police station for help.

- When driving, be alert to the signs of a drunk driver:

  ✓ Swerving and weaving

  ✓ Wide turns

  ✓ Driving to the left of center

  ✓ Driving in the dark with the headlights off

  ✓ Driving on the shoulder

  ✓ Unusual stopping

Visit *www.NaturalHomekeeping.com* for free tips, resources and information on maintaining a natural home and healthy life style.

$ Watching Your Pennies—Around Your Home $

*These suggestions count toward going green. Not only will they save you money, they are environmentally conscientious choices, as well.

✓ Lowering the thermostat even one degree saves money. Turn down the heat when you go to bed. *

✓ Contact your electric company and see if enrolling in load management, off-hour rate, or other cost-savings programs will save you money on electricity costs.

✓ If you live in a house or apartment where it is your responsibility to keep the heating and air conditioning filters clean, check them at least once every change of season. If they look dirty, replace them, as clean filters save money and energy. *

✓ Turn off the air conditioner if you'll be away for several hours. *

✓ When not in use, unplug small appliances that use "phantom" energy. *

✓ Turn off lights you're not really using. *

✓ Close the door to the fridge ASAP. *

✓ If you do not have an economy cycle on the dishwasher, skip the dry cycle. Let the dishes air dry. *

✓ Be mindful of how much water you are using and how you can cut down. For example, you might be able to shorten the time you spend in the shower and make it a point not to leave the water running while you brush your teeth. *

✓ Set your water heater to 120 degrees. *

✓ Cover water when you boil it. Not only is this more energy efficient, but the water will boil faster. *

✓ Consider carefully what cable and satellite services you sign up for. Will you really use those premium channels?

Related Reading:

Emergency Food Storage & Survival Handbook: Everything You Need to Know to Keep Your Family Safe in a Crisis by Peggy Layton. Clarkson Potter; 2012.

Go Green, Live Rich: 50 Simple Ways to Save the Earth and Get Rich Trying by David Bach and Hillary Rosner. Broadway; 2008.

Gorgeously Green: 8 Simple Steps to an Earth-Friendly Life by Sophie Uliano. Collins Living; 2008.

Hot, Flat, and Crowded 2.0: Why We Need a Green Revolution-and How It Can Renew America by Thomas L. Friedman. Picador; 2009.

How to Organize (Just About) Everything: More Than 500 Step-by-Step Instructions for Everything from Organizing Your Closets to Planning a Wedding to Creating a Flawless Filing System by Peter Walsh. Free Press; 2004.

Lighten Up: Love What You Have, Have What You Need, Be Happier with Less by Peter Walsh. Free Press; 2011.

Martha Stewart's Homekeeping Handbook: The Essential Guide to Caring for Everything in Your Home by Martha Stewart. Clarkson Potter; 2006.

Organize Now!: A Week-by-Week Guide to Simplify Your Space and Your Life by Jennifer Ford Berry. How; 2 edition; 2010.

Organized Simplicity: The Clutter-Free Approach to Intentional Living by Tsh Oxenreider. Betterway Home; 2010.

The Unthinkable: Who Survives When Disaster Strikes - and Why by Amanda Ripley. Three Rivers Press; 2009.

For information, news and tips on earth-friendly living visit *www.TheDailyGreen.com.*

Chapter 5

Maintaining the Basics

Staying on Top of It All

Successfully living on your own requires that you take good care of yourself, your home, your possessions, and your time. Order goes to chaos unless we expend the energy to maintain the order; and maintaining order and balance in life makes thriving, not just surviving, possible. It's hard to grow and really get the most out of life when you are continually bogged down in unnecessary situations that need attention. If you don't change the oil in your car, you will ultimately end up dealing with the inconvenience and the expense of repairs. If you don't maintain your health, you may suffer the inconvenience of an illness and the expense of medical bills. While you cannot control every aspect of your life, working at maintaining the basics will help you avoid living your life moving from one mini-crisis to another and will give you the freedom you need to enjoy the life you are building.

Your Home

Most people I know seem to have definite feelings regarding housework, ranging from fanatical obsession to absolute loathing, with almost everyone having very strong opinions about the best way to go about the chore. You, too, will find the way to maintain your place that works best for you. I recommend you just get the job done to your own satisfaction and do not even think about the "dusting before or after vacuuming" debate. No matter what your particular style of housecleaning may be, have a few cleaning supplies on hand:

Cleaning Supplies
- Bucket
- Clean rags
- Dishwashing liquid
- Dust cloth
- Glass cleaner
- Multipurpose cleaner
- Toilet brush
- Vacuum cleaner
- For cleaning non-carpeted floors, you might want one or more of these: broom, mop, and dust mop with washable head. Have at least one, especially if you do not have a vacuum cleaner.

Now might be a good time to decide what your commitment is to "going green." If saving the planet is on your to-do list, buying environmentally responsible products is one way you can contribute. By choosing less toxic cleaners than standard chemical household products, you are not only helping to curb harmful effects on the environment, you are also creating a healthier environment for yourself.

When using household cleaners, make sure to read the labels carefully. Never mix different cleaning products together. Sometimes combining products makes each individual product ineffective, but depending on the chemicals, mixing or using the wrong products together could create an extremely dangerous chemical reaction. Follow the instructions exactly.

It may be hard to believe, but there are some people who actually love to clean. They can't get enough of it. In case that does not sound like you, here's a reminder of the things that you should attend to regularly. Your lifestyle, dirt tolerance, and your definition of clean will dictate how often *regularly* is for you. If your home is a high traffic zone, you may need to clean more frequently than someone who spends most of their at-home time alone.

Regular Housecleaning

- Put away clutter
- Thoroughly clean kitchen
- Clean bathroom, including toilet and shower
- Vacuum floors
- Wash kitchen and bathroom floors
- Dust
- Change your sheets

Cranking up the music volume and cleaning your whole place at a break-neck pace may work great for you, or slowly, meditatively cleaning one room at a time may be more your style. Just get it done. Put off cleaning and you will just have a bigger mess to eventually take care of. Stay on top of your housework and you won't have to take large chunks of time out of your schedule to get the jobs finished.

Clutter. Your place can be clean but still look like a mess if you create mounds of clutter. Even the thought of picking the stuff up and putting it away will seem overwhelming. If you have things lying around in every room, you may want to take time the day before you do your housecleaning to deal with straightening up. Start with the things you have thrown on the floor and work your way up. Go room by room, putting things where they belong or find a better place to keep items if the place you had for them isn't working out.

Keep in mind that even though you may still be acquiring things you need for your place, there may be items you own that are no longer useful to you. Pass things along to your friends. Keep a bag or box handy in which to put items you no longer need. When it is full, give it to charity. Throw things away that are beyond use to anyone. Don't fall into the clutches of clutter.

Cleaning the Kitchen. This is the one room that really should be kept clean. It's so tempting to just leave the dishes, the sticky pots and pans, and the yucky stuff spilled on the bottom of the oven. Yet, if you do, you will find yourself spending your precious nonworking hours working hard—cleaning up a horrendous mess!

- Wipe up spills and put ingredients away as you cook.
- Wash down countertops with liquid detergent, hot water, and a clean dishcloth.
- Stay on top of the dirty dishes. If you only have a few dirty dishes to wash, you may want to wash them by hand instead of running the dish washer. If you have a dishwasher, always run full loads.
- Soak sticky pots and pans and wash them with the next round of dirty dishes. If the food is burned or baked on, try boiling water and a squirt of dishwasher detergent in the pan for several minutes to loosen the stain, then scrub the pan with non-abrasive scouring powder. You might need to repeat the process if necessary.
- Wipe appliances after you use them.
- Wipe up drips and dirt in the refrigerator before it starts to smell. Throw away anything that looks like a biology experiment.
- Wash the floor and empty the trash at least once a week.

Cleaning the Bathroom. Ick!

- Start with the countertop. Remove everything from the surface and wipe down with all purpose cleaner and hot water.
- Get the goop out of the soap dish.
- Scrub the tub/shower with cleanser or soap scum remover. Clean the glass shower doors. If you have a shower curtain, run it through the washer every month or two. If you use liquid bleach in your home, add a quarter cup to the wash cycle to help remove any mildew.

- Scrub the inside of the toilet bowl with a toilet brush; scrub the outside, the seat, and surrounding areas with multipurpose cleaner and hot water.
- Scrub the sink.
- Clean the mirror.
- Vacuum and wash the floor.

Vacuuming the Floors. Some vacuum cleaners have one attachment for cleaning noncarpeted surfaces and one attachment for vacuuming carpet. There are some vacuums that are for carpet only. Make sure you are aware of what you are buying. If you can vacuum the kitchen and bathroom floors before you wash them, you will find it's much, much easier. Use a broom or dust mop if you do not have a floor attachment.

- Vacuum as often as needed, but don't think you need to make a big deal out of it every time. Yet, several times a year, move all the furniture and vacuum every square inch of your place. You may want to purchase an allergen product to sprinkle on your carpet before you vacuum to help kill and remove dust mites.
- Keep extra vacuum bags on hand. Stopping in the middle of cleaning to run around town looking for the correct bag may get you totally out of the mood to continue with your efforts. Write the bag refill information in your organizer or planner.

Washing the Floors. Here's another area where people seem to have strong preferences—either toward using the mop or getting down on your hands and knees. Whatever you decide, use a cleaning product that is appropriate for the surface. Walk all the way into the room and work as you move backward, using hot water and a clean mop or cleaning rag. Scuff marks or stains may need to be scrubbed with non-abrasive scouring powder and then washed. You may need to go over the floor again with hot rinse water.

Hint: When you get sick and tired of keeping your floors clean and you want to cut down on the amount of vacuuming and washing you are doing, there is a painless solution. Kick your shoes off every time you walk in the door.

Shoes track in all the worst little bits of our world—not only dirt, but also germs, pesticides, and other toxins. People spit in parking lots and drip in public rest rooms. Businesses spray to control insects, and we all know what dogs do. We bring it all into our home every day on the bottom of our shoes.

Initiate a "no-shoes in the house" policy, and you will dramatically reduce the amount of pollutants in your home and the amount of time spent cleaning them up.

Dusting. There are those who swear it's best to dust before you vacuum because all the dust gets on the floor, and those who think it's best to dust after you vacuum because vacuuming creates more dust. Whatever side you join, you'll find dusting can make your place look better, and it's much healthier for you, too.

- If you use treated dustcloths, make sure they are appropriate for the type of furniture you have. Otherwise, use a cloth that does not leave behind lint. Old T-shirts work great.

- Generally you won't need more than a dustcloth to get the job done. You can easily ruin the finish on a piece of furniture by applying the wrong furniture cleaner. Be careful of spray furniture polish, as it can actually dull some shiny finishes. Furniture oil, although sometimes necessary to prevent wood from drying out, attracts dust. Furniture wax repels dust.

- Dust top to bottom—high shelf to low shelf.

- Pick up an item, dust it, dust where it was, and replace the item. When you do your more thorough cleaning, remove everything from the shelf or piece of furniture, dust each item, and clean and wax your furniture.

- Shake out the dustcloth often (outside).

Change Your Sheets. Please. If you have two sets of sheets, you can alternate. If you have a washer and dryer nearby, putting the same sheets back on your bed after you wash them will save you the trouble of folding them up. Always wash new sheets before use.

Less Frequent Chores. As I already mentioned, there are a few things that you will need to do *occasionally* in addition to your regular housecleaning. That's another subjective term that means different things to different people. You'll come up with your own definition of exactly how often *occasionally* is to you.

Occasional Chores

- Vacuum under the couch, bed, and behind the refrigerator
- Remove cobwebs from the ceiling and room corners
- Wash the windows and sills
- Wash your mattress cover
- Wash your shower curtain
- Wash any throw rugs
- Clean the refrigerator
- Clean the inside of the oven

Reminder: If you have a home computer, you will need to clean that, too. Use cleaning products that are designed specifically for computers. For instance, use compressed air to remove the dust from the keyboard, disk drive, and mouse.

Your Laundry

Even though I enjoy doing the laundry, I often tend to try to cut corners. When I'm too lazy to take the time to be more careful, I'm guilty of haphazard sorting, frenzily overstuffing the washer, and forgetful overdrying. And my clothes have paid the price of my carelessness. Ruin a couple of your favorite outfits and you'll agree that taking proper care of clothes helps them last longer and look better.

If you are fortunate enough not to use a coin washer and dryer, you can really dig into the world of correct clothes keeping. If you use a coin-operated washer and dryer, doing your laundry can get pretty expensive. You may want to limit the variations in your wardrobe to save on the number of different loads you have to wash. If you wear only t-shirts and jeans, you are not going to have a problem, but branch out into finicky fabrics and bold colors and you'll have to spend a little more time and money on the upkeep. Consider at least keeping all your towels in the same color group (light, bright, or dark) to prevent having to pay to wash several small loads.

Laundry Supplies

- Laundry detergent

Extras

- Bleach – Chlorine, and/or oxygen or other color safe bleach
- Fabric softener
- Iron
- Ironing board
- Stain remover – such as Spray 'N Wash, Shout, Oxi-Clean, or an instant stain remover stick or spray.

Sorting. The idea behind careful sorting is not to discolor, stretch, shrink, wrinkle, wear out, or wreck what you wash. You already know to separate the whites from the colors. Taking it further, you can sort not only by color, but also by weight, water temperature, and how much lint the item makes. For example:

- Delicates
- Whites and light colors
- Dark colors
- Bright colors (reds, etc.)

- Heavyweights (like jeans and sweat shirts)
- Towels (terry cloth robes, etc.)

That may be taking it a little far, but you get the idea. Sure, you can throw white towels in with a load of white clothes. Towels are listed separately because they tend to create lint and because they can be very heavy. If you are washing lightweight cotton blouses with heavy bath towels, you may end up doing a wee bit of ironing. The more experience you acquire, the more you'll learn just where you can and can't cut corners.

- Give wadded-up socks and clothes a shake before you throw them into the washer.
- Turn pockets inside out.
- Tie drawstrings and sashes to avoid wet tangles.

Hand Washing. If you have a hand wash cycle on your washer, you're set. Otherwise, it really is best to hand wash an item labeled "Hand Wash Only." Also, washing out a few things by hand may hold you over until you can get around to all of your laundry.

There are special detergents and soaps available for washing by hand, but you can also use just a little bit of your regular detergent. Read the product's label. Add the garment to the sudsy water. Be careful not to add the detergent directly to the item or it may spot. Swish and soak for a few minutes, then let the soapy water out, and fill the sink with rinse water. Swish some more, let the water out, and rinse the item thoroughly under running water. Be careful about not wringing and stretching delicate fabrics. Press the water out instead. When you are sure all the soap is out, fold the item in a dry towel and blot out the excess water.

Follow the garment's instructions about drying. "Line dry" means to hang it on a line or hanger to dry (a plastic hanger if you have one.) "Block" or "flat" means to lay it on a dry towel and try to arrange it back to what it looked like before it was washed.

Dry Cleaning. You may have clothes with care labels that read "Dry Clean Only." Generally, garments labeled "Dry Clean Only" really mean dry clean only. This is usually because at least part of the garment is not washable. You may have more leeway with care labels *recommending* "Dry Clean." If you are tempted to wash any of your dry clean garments—for instance something silk, cotton, or linen—make sure the item does not have interfacing, lining, or complicated construction. Dab a small hidden area with a wet cloth to make sure the color is not going to run. Hand wash in cold water. When money is tight, stay away from "Dry Clean *Only*" garments.

Laundry Detergent. This is the one essential laundry supply you need. You may want to use the same brand you are used to or experiment with the ones you find on sale.

- Liquid detergents are usually better on greasy stains; powder detergents work best on the muddy ones.

- While it's best to follow the recommended instructions for the detergent you are using, you will soon figure out the correct amount of detergent that works best for your water type. If you add too much, it won't all rinse out, and you'll find that your laundry is stiff with detergent buildup. If you don't add enough, the lint and dirt will not lift out and your laundry will not get clean.

- Buy a detergent designed to work best in the water temperature you use most often.

- First, let the washer begin to fill, then add the detergent. Next, add the clothes. Some detergents will spot fabrics if they are not dissolved first.

Stains. Most spills and spots need some type of immediate attention or they will never come completely out.

- There are several products available to treat stains before they are washed. If you buy one that does not require you to wash the garment right away, you can treat the article and let it sit until it's washed. These prewash products work especially well on greasy stains like butter, oil, and lipstick.

- Enzyme detergents, such as Wisk or Biz, are good for soaking protein stains, such as grass, blood, and egg.
- Muddy clothes may need to be treated with a stain remover and soaked in detergent before being washed.
- Lemon juice and vinegar are both mild bleaches. Mix one part juice or vinegar with one part water. This should remove the color left behind by most stains.

Bleach. Chlorine bleach is used to keep whites bright—yet, not *all* whites. Be sure to read labels carefully before you bleach anything. If you do not have a bleach dispenser, add the bleach after the wash cycle has started. Never pour bleach onto dry clothes. It must be diluted before it hits the fabric. Only use chlorine bleach on your whites occasionally, since the bleach will weaken the fabric.

- Use only color safe or all fabric bleach on colored fabrics.

Machine Settings.

Permanent Press: Use this cycle for normal loads. It adds cool water to the load before it spins to reduce wrinkles.

Regular Cycle: This cycle is best for heavy, sturdy, and very dirty loads.

Delicate Cycle: This cycle is for lightweight and loosely woven fabrics.

Clothes need room to move around in the washer. A load of laundry should fill the washer three-quarters of the way full. Overstuffing the washer will also set in wrinkles.

Water Temperature.

Hot—best for keeping whites bright
Warm—average loads
Cold—bright colors and delicate fabrics

Fabric Softener. Liquid softener is added during the rinse cycle and fabric softener sheets are put into the dryer.

- If your washer does not have an automatic dispenser, dilute the fabric softener with warm water and add to the rinse water. Do not pour it directly onto any fabric since it can cause spots.

- Fabric softener can also build up in your laundry. If your laundry begins to feel slippery and look dingy, cut down on fabric softener. Use it only every few washes.

- Don't use fabric softener on your kitchen towels and dishcloths.

- If you have asthma or allergies, check with your doctor before using dryer fabric softener sheets. An unscented brand is available if your allergy is to fragrance.

Drying. Clean the lint filter after every load. This will cut down on the drying time and allow the dryer to be more energy efficient.

- Shake out each item as you take it from the washer.

- Heat from the dryer will really set a stain, so make sure treated spots and stains have washed out. Retreat and re-wash any stain that's still noticeable.

- Hang up delicate items and those with elastic.

- Do not overload the dryer; it will cause your clothes to wrinkle.

- Shake out sheets and pillowcases at least once during the drying cycle to avoid them drying in a ball, with some parts remaining damp.

- Follow the care label's drying instructions. Often, the dryer will shrink fabrics, so be very careful not to get clothes too hot.

- Overdrying will cause your clothes to fade. Remove clothes when they are just dry.

The Laundromat. If you have a shared laundry room where you live, or if you go to the local laundromat, here are a few extra things to keep in mind:

- Find out if there is a time when the laundry room is normally not crowded. I have a cousin who does her laundry on the same day each week—at four o'clock in the morning—but she never has to wait for a machine!
- Sort all your loads before you get there. Put each load in a plastic bag and use your laundry baskets for transferring clean clothes from the washer to the dryer, and for bringing the clean laundry home.
- Check the washer for anything left over from previous use before you add your clothes. You may need to wipe a machine out before using.
- Make sure you don't leave any leftovers in the washer or dryer.
- Do not leave your laundry sitting in a machine. Be courteous to others who also use the facilities.

Ironing. This task is definitely not as popular as it used to be. If you have items that must be ironed, remove them from the dryer while they are still a little damp.

- Familiarize yourself with your iron. Use the correct setting for the material you are ironing. When in doubt, start with a low setting and move up to a higher or hotter one if necessary.
- Cotton and permanent press fabrics can tolerate quite a bit of moisture and steam. This makes removing wrinkles much easier. Use a spray bottle filled with warm water if you need more moisture than your iron's steam setting provides. Use distilled water in your iron to prevent mineral deposits.
- Iron with the grain of the fabric, back and forth, not in a circular motion.

- Allow the fabric of the area you are ironing to cool a few seconds, to set the press, before you move on to another area.

- On hard to press items, try using spray sizing or a light spray starch.

- If you really hate to iron, press only the parts of the garment that are going to show.

Sewing Kit. Buttons fall off, seams rip, and pockets mysteriously develop holes. Yet, you'll be able to fix the problem in just a couple of minutes if you have the basic sewing tools available:

- All purpose thread: Buy a few of the basic colors that are in your wardrobe.

- Dual-duty thread: Heavy-duty thread used to sew on buttons. You may want a couple of small spools.

- Needles: Buy a package of assorted sizes.

- Pin cushion

- Pins – safety and straight

- Sewing scissors: Use this pair for cutting fabric and thread only. Label them "Fabric Only" with a permanent marker. They will never be the same if you use them to cut paper.

- Seam ripper: Use to remove stitches easily, like when a button falls off and leaves a clump of thread behind.

- Tape measure: The soft fabric or paper kind. You may be surprised at how often you'll use this.

Hint: If you have thread leftover in the needle, save the needle in your pin cushion. You'll be that much more prepared for your next sewing emergency.

Your Shoes. Shoes? Yes! Don't underestimate the importance of the appearance of your shoes. People notice, especially if you are working in the business arena. To keep your shoes well-maintained you'll need:

Shoe Care Supplies

- Flannel cloth for buffing
- Leather conditioner
- Shoe cleaning brush

- Leather cleaner
- Polish
- Soft cotton cloths

If you are not really into taking the time to clean your shoes the traditional way, there are one-step shoe care products available, such as disposable shoe shine wipes or polishing pads that do it all. Pick these up at discount stores.

Don't forget about your athletic shoes. Clean them before the stains are set for life.

Your Car

Getting your first car is exciting! No matter what it looks like, there's a certain thrill involved; a certain independence. Having your own transportation may open up a whole new world for you. Whether it's old or new, practice preventative maintenance with your car to keep it running safely.

Here are a few things to keep in mind. Cars require all of the following fluids which need to be checked for levels and leaks:

- Battery
- Coolant (antifreeze)
- Power steering
- Windshield washer

- Brake
- Engine oil
- Transmission

With the convenience of fast, economical servicing facilities, or quick lubes, you may not want to actually do the labor yourself; but you do need to make sure to take the car in to have the regular servicing done. Your owner's manual outlines a maintenance schedule you should follow. If you do not have an owner's manual, call the manufacturer of the car for the information. Some quick lubes "top off" fluids between visits free of charge. Or, you can always pull into a full-service gas station and ask the attendant to check under the hood. Or, of course you can learn to do it yourself!

Also Check:

- Battery
- Brakes
- Tires

- Belts and hoses
- Filters
- Windshield wiper blades

Battery. Not only does the battery require a fluid check, but also a check to ensure it has the proper charge and that the terminals are free from corrosion.

Belts and Hoses. Belts need to be checked for wear and proper tightness. Hoses need to be free from bulges and cracks. Check at every oil change.

Brakes. Have your brakes checked according to your car manufacturer's suggested schedule, or sooner if you sense a problem such as a pull in either direction when you press the brake or having to press the pedal down further to the floor.

Hint: Anticipate stop signs and signals. Slow down gradually. Zooming from one red light to the next shortens the life of your brakes as well as wastes gas.

Filters. Your car has both fuel and air filters. They should be checked with every oil change. If you are told you need a new filter, look at the filter to determine whether you really do or not. Cabin air filters should be changed at least once a year.

Tires.

- Check your owner's manual for the proper amount of air pressure.
- Tires need to be rotated and aligned on a regular basis, generally every 6,000 to 8,000 miles. Your car pulling to one side or starting to jiggle at certain speeds could be an indication that the tires are out of balance.
- Tires are legally bald when there is less than one-sixteenth of an inch of tread remaining.

Windshield Wiper Blades. Check blades twice a year. Replace if you notice streaking or signs of splitting or cracking.

Car Trouble. The more you learn about maintaining your car, the less dependent you will be on others. You will also be more in touch with your car and better able to detect and avoid car trouble. Cars often give early warning signs of upcoming problems. The Car Care Council offers a list of common signs. Here are a few:

- More often than before, you're finding it necessary to add oil between changes.

- There is a squealing or scraping sound when you apply the brakes.

- You hear knocks and pings from the engine when you accelerate or climb a hill.

- There is a rumbling or hissing sound coming from your muffler.

- Your engine keeps chugging after you've turned off the ignition.

Repairs. When your car needs more help than you know how to give, you'll need to find an automotive repair shop. This is another time when it's good to ask around for recommendations from family and friends. Someone may know a shop that does excellent work at reasonable prices, which is exactly what you are looking for.

- Look for professional certifications, such as from: the National Institute for Automotive Service Excellence, the American Automobile Association, or the Automotive Service Council.

- The shop you choose should give you a free estimate of the repair costs and obtain your approval before starting to work on the car.

- The shop should be willing to work with you. This means they should be courteous, listen to your explanation of why you think the car needs attention, and understand when you need to have the repairs completed.

- If the shop discovers additional work that needs to be performed which was not included in the original estimate, the shop should provide you with an estimate of the extra work and obtain your approval before starting the additional repairs.

- The shop should give you written invoices for the repairs, labor, and parts.

- Just as with getting a diagnosis from your doctor, it is reasonable for you to seek a second opinion concerning the diagnosis of your car. If your gut instinct tells you to go somewhere else, then do so.

- Your local Better Business Bureau and Consumer Affairs agency will be able to tell you if there is a significant history of complaints and disciplinary actions against a shop.

Hint: Keep a file about your car. Include a dated service record and the receipts for all service and repairs.

Keeping Your Car Clean. Salt, grime, bugs, bird droppings, sap, and air pollution can all have damaging effects on your car's paint, which can lead to body rot. You may want to take your car to an automated car wash or save some money and wash it yourself. Here are some suggestions for washing your car by hand:

- Buy a liquid detergent specifically designed for washing cars. Dishwashing liquid can strip car wax.

- Wash the wheels first.

- Hose the entire car, top to bottom, with medium stream pressure.

- Gently clean the roof, trunk, and hood. Use a car wash mitt, sponge, or *soft* cotton cloths. Wring and rinse out frequently.
- Rinse each area when finished.
- Clean the sides, bumper, and grill.
- Rinse.
- Use clean, dry, lint-free cloths or a synthetic chamois to *blot* the car dry.
- Open the doors, hood, and trunk to wipe up any water that leaked in.
- Vacuum the interior.
- Clean the inside windows and rearview mirror.
- Wipe down the inside surfaces with a clean damp cloth.

Car Keeping Hints:

- If you notice bird droppings or sap on your paint, wash the spot off right away; don't wait until the next car wash.
- Keep your headlights clean between washings. Dirt diminishes their effectiveness.
- Wax your car by hand at least a couple of times a year. Buy a good quality wax and follow the directions on the label.

Car Supplies. Here are two lists of supplies you should have in your car. The first list of items should be kept in your trunk. Use a plastic storage container, a duffel bag, or tote to keep everything together. The second list is for supplies you may want to have on hand inside the passenger compartment. Items inside the passenger compartment should always be kept secured, for example, in the glove compartment.

Car Safety Supplies—Trunk

- Blanket
- Can of instant puncture seal
- Flashing, battery-operated emergency light
- Jumper cables
- Reflector triangle
- Spray window cleaner and paper towels
- Tire jack
- Water (in a plastic bottle or jug)

Seasonal

- Small bag of sand, cat box filler, or rock salt.

Car Supplies—Inside

- Car's owner manual
- Change for parking and tolls
- First aid kit (including motion sickness medication— for a passenger, *not* for the driver)
- Flashlight
- Map
- Paper and note pad
- Proof of insurance and registration
- Trash bags
- Umbrella

Seasonal

- Snow brush/ice scraper
- Sun screen
- Spray de-icer (can)
- Sun shield

Important: A loose item rolling under the accelerator or brake can be a potentially dangerous situation. Loose items can also be extremely damaging in an accident. Put small items in the glove or other compartment. Buy a behind-the-front-seat organizer if your car does not provide storage space.

> If you do not already know how to jump-start a car or change a tire, please take the time now to learn.

For additional information visit:

www.CarCare.org   *www.ConsumerReports.org*
www.KBB.com   *www.RoadAndTravel.com*

Your Well-Being

I've been telling you what to do—and what not to do—for over five chapters now. Of all the information in this book, the single thing I hope you will most incorporate into your life is: *Take care of yourself—physically, emotionally, mentally, and spiritually.*

It's easy not to give our health much attention when we are well. Yet, in my opinion, we need to be attentive to our health or we will not *stay* well. Without meaning to, we can do ourselves a disservice. Have you ever been tired beyond belief only to realize that you either haven't been eating much, or eating all the wrong things? Or have you ever been surprised at how irritable you feel, only later to realize how much stress and strain you were living under? Paying close attention to all aspects of your health, or wellness, will help keep your life in balance. It's much harder to live life to its fullest when you are not caring for your wellness.

Life requires a certain amount of energy from you each day. You have to find that energy somewhere or you will be operating from a deficit position—which means, clearly not at your best.

Since we are all wonderfully different, we all seem to have different ways to keep going and remain energized. Even though the specifics of what it takes to keep us well and running at our best are different, we all share common ways to become energized and to care for our wellness:

Wellness Watch

- Nourishment
- Sleep
- Exercise
- Lifestyle
- Indulgences

Nourishment. The next chapter will be entirely devoted to food because it's so important in your life, or should be. Do you remember the analogy we learned in grade school about how the body needs food just like a car needs gas? Well, I guess it has been around for generations because it's so true. We have to have nourishment to keep our bodies energized.

You've seen the charts of the food pyramid and what you are supposed to eat. Do you know anyone who actually eats the recommendations *every single day?* It's a goal we all need to shoot for. If you had trouble eating right before, use living on your own as an opportunity to take charge of your nutritional intake. Please don't fall into the routine of not feeding yourself well. It is tempting not to take the time and the trouble to prepare yourself wholesome meals. You may even feel a little silly about fixing a full meal, with a nice table setting, to enjoy all by yourself. Yet, your well-being is certainly worth the effort.

You may want to take vitamin and mineral supplements to ensure you at least receive the basic nutrients your body needs. If you do, please be mindful that vitamins and minerals should be supplements to, and not substitutes for, whole food.

- Eat a variety of different foods and food combinations. Eating the same things over and over is not only boring, but is also not as healthy as enjoying all the wonderful foods that are available to us.

- Everyone has time to eat. If you are spending your life with no time for meals, you need to do whatever you have to do to fix the situation. Eat!

- If you use the excuse that you don't like cooking for just one person, cook several servings and freeze the excess in individual containers that you can heat up another time.
- Invite people over for meals. Friends will enjoy and appreciate even the simplest meal.
- Cooking actually is part art and part science. Give it a try. You may find cooking to be a way to relax or possibly to be your creative outlet. You may discover you have a gift!

Sleep. While the effects of poor eating habits may not be apparent immediately, the effects of poor sleep habits become apparent right away. We can feel terrible, can act terrible, and can even get in terrible accidents when we are suffering from sleep deprivation. Living on your own may mean you can sleep whenever you choose, but your body clock is going to have its say.

The benefits of sleep are not cumulative: Get a good night's sleep and you may feel strong enough to push yourself and cut back on several hours the next night. Well, that's where the trouble starts. You are going to feel tired if you do not maintain an overall reasonable amount of rest for your body.

Your lifestyle should accommodate your sleep requirements and sleep patterns. You know how many hours of sleep work best for you, and rarely is it a good idea to skip or scrimp on getting the amount you need. Uninterrupted sleep is the best. Turn off the ringer on the phone if you have to. Say no to a social invitation if what you really want is a solid night's sleep. Put extra covering over your bedroom window if you sleep best in an absolutely dark room. Fix your environment and your timetable to get every bit of sleep you crave.

There are those among us who live to sleep. Whatever your unique sleep patterns are, if you notice a prolonged increase or decrease in your sleep time, you may want to talk to your doctor.

Exercise. Isn't it odd that an antidote to fatigue can be exercise? If you've ever been the kind of tired that has nothing to do with how much sleep you get, you understand why I think it's odd. Pushing yourself to exercise when you feel fatigued can take a tremendous amount of energy—even just talking yourself into it can take energy!

The American Cancer Society (*www.cancer.org*) and the American Heart Association (*www.AmericanHeart.org*) recommend at least thirty minutes of moderate to vigorous activity at least five days a week.

You may need to do some searching to find the activities that are right for you. Sticking with exercise is much harder if you're not enjoying what you are doing. You may want to enlist the support of a friend or coworker to help you keep up with your exercise routine. Knowing you have a standing meeting to work out with a friend may be all you need to keep on track. Try doing a 'sneaker switch' with your friend to help insure that you won't break your appointment.

Lifestyle. Well, this word is certainly thrown around a lot, isn't it? Your lifestyle, or your typical approach to living, affects all aspects of your happiness and well-being. Living a life that goes strongly against your heartfelt and soulful desires can be a painful existence. We all make lifestyle choices. Sometimes our choices enhance our lives, sometimes the choices hinder our well-being. Stay in touch with how the choices you make affect you.

When your lifestyle replenishes your inner vitality, you will be at your best. Not only will you feel better, but you will also have the energy to grow into an interesting and productive individual. We all experience times when we feel out of balance, when parts of our lives just aren't working. It can sap our strength straight out of us. Those are the times when we need to examine our lifestyle and see what areas need attention. Are we trying to accommodate the desires of too many other people? Are negative personal habits draining our energy? Pinpointing areas where we can positively change will go a long way to keeping us happy and healthy.

Finding something you love and are passionate about has long been a great energizer. When you incorporate that passion into your daily life, you will find vitality. If you do not have something you are enthusiastic about, the process of searching for that something can in itself be a wonderful experience. Keep learning and developing interests in different things. You may find that passion, and you will definitely turn into a more interesting and well-rounded person.

> Live the lifestyle that suits you best; adjust areas that do not serve you. Make the effort to choose a lifestyle that enhances your well-being.

Indulgences. I've heard it said that there is more to life than just being comfortable, and while I agree, being comfortable (in comfort's most luxurious sense) is to me, about as good as it gets. A hot shower and putting on my favorite old clothes goes a long way toward maintaining my wellness.

The little ways we treat ourselves matter as much as the major life decisions we make. You may need to indulge yourself a bit while you are living on your own. Of course, I am not talking about negative indulgences here. I am talking about being nice to yourself. Do what it takes to keep yourself happy and content. Hopefully, when you're happy it will rub off on the other people in your life.

Stress may be an issue for you. Perhaps you are trying to excel and advance in your job. You may be carrying the additional responsibility of trying to get an education while working. You may feel stressed and overwhelmed by your new world of being an independent person. Being tender to yourself may help you keep the stress at bay and revitalize your spirit.

Indulge yourself once in awhile. Make sure, though, that it is not an indulgence that will *cause* stress in another area of your life. For example, don't rationalize indulging yourself with a major purchase you can't afford when you'll end up creating a stressful financial situation.

Be kind to yourself. Don't constantly push yourself too hard. Push yourself when you know you can handle the consequences. Now that you are on your own, do things you have always wanted to do. Find positive little ways to make life work for you, even if it's as simple as making your favorite cookies and taking a nice long nap.

Depression. Successfully living on your own requires responsibility in all areas of your life. If you start to feel overwhelmed with all your new responsibilities, seek out assistance. If loneliness becomes a constant feeling, get help. If you think you may be experiencing depression, not just a case of "the blues," see your doctor. Depression takes many forms, but a few of the symptoms include:

- Being sad, worried, irritable, and having little or no interest in the things that used to give you pleasure.
- Negative thoughts; difficulty concentrating and making decisions.
- Feelings of hopelessness, anxiety, or fear.
- Changes in sleep patterns, appetite, or weight.
- Thoughts of harming yourself or others.

We all go through periods when we are not operating at our best and can use some help. Please don't ever hesitate to ask for assistance.

The Doctor. Regardless of how attentive you are to your well-being, there will still be occasions when you will need to visit the doctor. Having a regular doctor who tracks your history, a doctor that you are comfortable with and that you have confidence in, can be a real blessing.

There are referral agencies that will help you find a doctor. Do a search for "Physician, General Practitioner." Here again, it may be a good idea to talk to your family, friends, and coworkers about their experiences with their physicians. Even if you have a medical plan that dictates which doctors you see, there may be several doctors available in the group.

Have you ever felt too sick to go to the doctor? While living on your own, there may come a time when you will need to determine carefully whether you are sick enough to see the doctor. Hopefully, you will see a doctor before you are so sick you can't get out of bed. Don't be reluctant to get a family member or a friend's opinion as to how sick you are. Often we tend to think we're not as ill as we really are and neglect getting timely treatment. Even a common illness like the flu can lead to secondary infections, such as bronchitis and life-threatening pneumonia. You need to take an illness seriously.

Know the difference between the flu and a cold. The flu usually hits you hard all at once, whereas you can feel a cold "coming on," with symptoms normally building up gradually. The flu usually includes a higher fever than a cold, more body aches, and possibly severe fatigue. Having over-the-counter medications on hand will prevent you from needing to shop when you feel awful.

Taking good care of yourself when you are sick will help reduce the chance of secondary infections. Your immune system needs all the help you can give. Get lots of rest and drink plenty of liquids. Do not hesitate to call the doctor.

- It is reasonable for you to expect your doctor to listen to all of your concerns.

- Ask direct questions and give direct and detailed answers to all questions your physician asks.

- Ask for detailed explanations of anything you do not understand.

- Do not be shy about taking notes. It's easy to forget what was said before you reach the parking lot.

If you can not afford to see a private doctor, check your phone book, or visit *www.ask.hrsa.gov* for the location of the closest public health clinic.

Hint: Fortunately, one of the most effective ways to prevent getting sick is also one of the easiest things to do—wash your hands—often. When you pick up germs from infected surfaces, you infect yourself when you touch your mouth, nose, and eyes.

According to the Centers for Disease Control and Prevention, frequent hand washing goes a long way in preventing the spread of infectious diseases. Check out their web site for additional helpful information: *www.cdc.gov.*

The Dentist. Some people don't mind going to the dentist, but some of us put it off until we are in the throngs of a dental crisis. Don't we already have enough to do?

According to the American Dental Association we are supposed to visit the dentist regularly for an examination and professional cleaning. The dentist looks not only for cavities, but also for other dental and medical problems, such as oral cancer.

There are referral agencies specifically for dentists. Whether you do an online search or check your local phone book, be sure to ask around for good referrals.

Your Time

Everyone's time is valuable. We've all had experiences in which we felt we were wasting our time, or worse, felt frustrated that someone else was wasting our time. Manage your time well and the benefits can be enormous.

Have you ever heard the adage that goes something like, "Ask a busy person to do something for you and it will get done; but ask someone who seems to have all the time in the world, and it will never get done"?

Some people have learned the skills involved with effective time management better than others. Some have learned time management skills, but are not time-integrated, and they are slaves to clocks, schedules, and a time-driven pace. When you have made peace with yourself regarding your use of your time, you will naturally set and be comfortable with your *own* pace, spending your time wisely.

One area that often trips us up is that we commit to things that we really do not want to do. We say "yes" instead of doing everyone a favor and saying "no." *Every commitment that you make is one that you should keep,* so use discretion when committing your time. Be in control of your time. For example, you may want to tell friends not to wake you up if they drop over, see your lights out, and know that you've gone to bed. You may want to discourage drop-by company altogether. The idea is for you to be in charge of exactly how you spend your time.

Procrastination. Some people need the pressure of a deadline to actually get a project accomplished; therefore, they wait until the last minute so they can catch that rush which fuels them to get the job done. Sound familiar? Putting things off until the last minute is not necessarily a bad thing. Sometimes it works. Yet, things are generally much easier and run smother when we face what we have to do and get it over with, dropping the excuses. There may never be the perfect time to make that phone call or write that letter.

Often the price of not doing the thing we are thinking about doing is so marginal we subconsciously think it doesn't matter anyway. If that is true in your case, if the cost of not doing it *truly* doesn't matter, maybe you are focusing your energy in the wrong direction to begin with.

Putting things off becomes a real problem when the task involved is one that gets bigger as time goes by. Leave the housecleaning for a couple of months and you will have a huge undertaking ahead of you. It's much easier to face a small task than an overwhelming one. It's easier to break a large task into manageable bits. It's also easier to spend the time it takes to do whatever you need to do, than to waste your time worrying about getting it done.

Errands. Running errands is one area in which a small amount of planning can save you a large amount of time. Thinking ahead, not only about what needs to be done, but also when and where, will really save you from time wasted dashing about.

- Remember that "cubby" area mentioned in Chapter 4? Pile up the library books, outgoing mail, dry cleaning to be dropped off, and so forth into one space. This will prevent you from having to search around for items you need to have with you. Consider using a tote bag.

- Group your errands by location and do them in logical order. Zig-zagging around takes additional time.

- If you are fortunate enough to live close to a facility that offers several services, try it out. Shopping for your groceries where you can drop off your dry cleaning, and medical prescriptions, as well as rent a movie, has got to be a time-saver.

- Anticipate your future needs. Are you low on, but not completely out of, stamps? If you are at the post office mailing a package anyway, buying stamps then will save you the additional trip. Buy some gas while you are out running errands, not when you are late for work.

- Keep pick-up slips from the dry cleaners, etc., in your car.

- Does something really require a special trip out or can you wait until you have an additional errand?

Free Time. It's wonderful to spend time as you genuinely desire. Even spending your free time doing nothing at all, on occasion, can be using it wisely. Do not let the demands of living on your own chew up all your free time. Become well-organized and a good manager of your time, even the small amounts. For example, find a way to make your lunch hour revitalizing. A change of scenery, a short nap, or a brisk walk may make a huge contribution to the rest of your day. Yes, you will need to keep up with maintaining your home, health, laundry, and car, but you also need to truly enjoy the time you call your own.

You might want to check out:

Home Economics by Jennifer Mcknight Trontz. Quirk Books; 2010.

Homegrown and Handmade: A Practical Guide to More Self-Reliant Living by Deborah Niemann. New Society Publishers; 2011.

The Urban Homestead (Expanded & Revised Edition): Your Guide to Self-Sufficient Living in the Heart of the City by Kelly Coyne and Erik Knutzen. Process; 2010.

Chapter 6

Eating In And Dining Out

Managing Your Meals

We think about food every day. We need to earn the money to pay for it, and we need to shop for it, cook it, and clean up after it's prepared. Food is such a large and continuous part of a normal day that if we aren't careful, eating can turn into a big monotonous chore. So big, in fact, that supermarkets are full of ready-to-eat individual meal servings, cleaned and ready-to-use ingredients, and hundreds of packaged, processed short-cuts to preparing meals—all designed to make meal preparation easy for us. What could be less hassle than sticking a complete frozen dinner in the microwave?

Your lifestyle will influence your eating patterns. How much time and money you have to spend will affect the choices you make. Although some of your monthly expenses are fixed amounts, such as your rent, the amount you spend on food each month can vary. You may need to stick to some no-frills cooking at home when funds are tight and visit your favorite restaurant or buy the gourmet foods when you can better afford to do so. Fortunately, there is quite a range of options available to us when it comes to purchasing our food. This is one area where we can easily go financially overboard, or where we can eat well very reasonably.

Variety is important when it comes to food. Even your favorite meals will become tiring if you eat them too often. Have you ever ordered take-out pizza so much you got sick of it? It's also nice not to prepare all your own meals every single day. Going to a restaurant, to a friend's or relative's house for a meal, or cooking for someone else, can be a refreshing break. Try not to fall into a rut when it comes to your eating habits. If you give yourself an assortment of food options and make wise choices both in cooking at home and in eating out, you should have no problem managing your meals while living on your own.

Cooking at Home

Turning empty kitchen cupboards into a well-stocked, serviceable pantry is not difficult, but it can be expensive. You may need to spread the cost out over several pay periods. Buy basic items first and add to your supplies when you can afford to do so. For example, you will probably use salt and pepper before you'll use cloves or sage.

Always have back-up food available. A few standards, like peanut butter, pasta, pasta sauce, canned tuna (low-mercury), or packaged soup, will get you through in a pinch. An extra loaf of bread in the freezer may save you a special trip to the store.

In addition to the fresh food that you like to eat, such as fruit, vegetables, meat, and bread, keep the basic provisions on hand. Adjust the following lists to fit your tastes:

Food Shopping List—The Basics

For the refrigerator:

- Butter
- Eggs
- Milk
- Cheese
- Juice
- Yogurt

For the freezer:

- Extra loaf of bread
- Frozen vegetables

For the pantry:

- Baking mix, all purpose, such as Bisquick
- Baking soda
- Beans (canned or dry)

- Cereal (ready to eat or oatmeal, hot-grain, etc.)
- Coffee and/or tea
- Condiments (such as ketchup, mayonnaise and mustard)
- Cooking oil- canola, coconut or vegetable and/or olive oil (buy small containers—oil turns rancid in a couple of months)
- Dried pasta and/or noodles
- Flour (store in an air-tight container, in a dark, dry place)
- Garlic
- Onions
- Peanut butter
- Pepper
- Potatoes
- Quinoa
- Rice
- Salt
- Soup (dry or canned)
- Sugar (store in an air-tight container)
- Syrup and/or honey
- Vinegar

Extras:

- Baking powder (small—keep tightly covered)
- Bouillon cubes
- Brown sugar (store in air-tight container or freeze)
- Cinnamon
- Crackers
- Jelly
- Paprika
- Tobasco Sauce
- Cocoa
- Dried herbs
- Nuts and/or raisins
- Soy Sauce
- Vanilla extract

Now is a great time to take control over what you eat and how you shop. Consider committing to only health-enhancing food, less packaging, and fewer chemicals and preservatives. The inexpensive book *Food Rules: An Eater's Manual* by Michael Pollan is a good place to start learning about what food choices to make.

Shopping. If you plan to cook at home, you will spend some time in the supermarket. Since you will consistently spend your hard-earned money there, it only makes sense to take the time to learn how to be a savvy grocery shopper, whether you are shopping for food or nonfood items. You may already be familiar with some of the following suggestions. Just make sure you remember them as you do your marketing.

- Shop to control your diet. Not diet as in weight-loss; but diet, as in your daily food and nutrition intake. Every food you eat will affect you. You know what foods you are supposed to eat: fruits, vegetables, grains, and legumes. Simply put, these foods affect you positively. You also know that high-fat, high-sugar foods can affect you negatively and that they should be avoided or consumed in moderation. Buy the foods you need to maintain a healthy diet.

- Buy ingredients. If you look at an item and it doesn't look like anything you've ever seen in nature, chances are good you should buy something else instead. Heavily processed, convenience foods are more expensive and may not be the healthiest choice. Another thing to be aware of is that buying prewashed, peeled, and packaged food is going to be more expensive. That little convenience of buying preshredded cheese is going to cost you more money.

- Plan your trips to the market. Let as much time pass as possible between visits. Dashing to the store three nights a week is not only an ineffective use of your time, but you also run the risk of impulsively buying items you don't really need. It's common to go to the store to pick up one thing and walk out with a grocery bag full of things you had no intention of buying. Supermarket managers are well aware of consumers' inclinations. Look at how a supermarket is laid out. The milk is almost always way at the back of the store so you will have to pass just about everything to get that half gallon you need. The most expensive items are the ones that are the easiest to see and reach. The checkout is loaded with appealing little extras, like candy and magazines, that are just waiting to accompany you home. One long trip to the store is more effective than several smaller ones.

- Always shop for groceries when you are alone. You will shop more efficiently.

- Always shop from a well-thought-out list. Resist the temptation to add items that are not on your list, *except* for items that you regularly use which happen to be on sale that visit. For instance, if you see your favorite bath soap is substantially discounted, you should grab a few bars because you know you will eventually use it. Take advantage of special prices on the items that you normally use. When preparing your list, group items together that are in the same area of the store. This will make shopping easier by preventing time-consuming backtracking.

- Buy only the food you know you will eat. This sounds too obvious, yet most of us, at one time or another, have been guilty of throwing food away. If you know you have a demanding week ahead of you, buying the fresh ingredients to make complicated recipes may not be the right thing to do. The food can go bad before you have the time to prepare the meals. Also, don't buy anything you really don't like. Chances are good that you will end up throwing it away when you could have substituted it for something you do enjoy, that is just as nutritious.

- Consider trying store brands when they are cheaper. You may find you like them just as well. Experiment with a small size first to find out if you like the product. Do not buy a large box of Brand X breakfast cereal before you know whether or not you will eat it all.

- Pay attention to price, volume, and count. The larger size is often the most economical, but not always.

- Use coupons for items that you *normally* buy. Sure, try a different brand name if you have a coupon, but do not buy something you won't normally use just because it's a few cents off.

- If you have environmental concerns, buy products with the least amount of packaging. Look for flexible packaging, such as bags and pouches, and concentrated items that require less packaging.

- The grocery store is the place to buy your snacks and soda, not the convenience store. Nearly everything will cost more in a convenience store. Plan ahead. Buy snacks to keep in your car if it will prevent you from stopping at a convenience store when you are out driving around.

- Select the cold food last, go straight home, and put it away immediately.

- Perhaps most importantly, don't shop for food when you are hungry. Eat before you go to the store. You'll save money.

- Store reusable grocery bags or totes in your vehicle so they are always on hand when you do your marketing.

Storage. Just as you made decisions on how to organize your kitchen items, you will also need to arrange your food to make cooking manageable. You are working against yourself if you have to hunt and dig for something you think you may have . . . somewhere. Unlike kitchen tools, food eventually spoils, so don't bury anything too deep.

- Whether it's dry groceries or cold stuff, group like things together.

Baking Supplies. Find a cool, dark, dry place to put flour, sugar, and so on. Once opened, these items need to be stored in an airtight container such as a large Ziploc storage bag, plastic storage container, canister, or jar. This is also where you can store your pasta, rice, and grains. Keep them away from a heat source, like the dishwasher or oven.

Oil/Spices/Seasonings. Here again, it's important to keep these items away from heat. They will last longer and not lose their flavor as quickly. A little cupboard next to the stove or oven may be convenient, but not ideal if it gets hot when the oven is on. Check to see if the cupboard warms up when you use the oven. If you live alone, buy small quantities of oil as it can go rancid before you have a chance to use it all.

General Items. Organizing like foods together on the shelf will not only make getting to your food easier, but will also help in preparing your shopping list. You can see at a glance that you are out of pasta sauce if the spot where you normally store it is empty. If you buy multiples of any item, make sure you use the older one first.

Produce. Potatoes, onions, garlic, and anything else that does not need to be refrigerated should also be stored in a cool, dry spot away from sunlight.

Refrigerator. The refrigerator should be 40 degrees or less. Arrange items not only for your convenience, but also as to not interfere with air circulation. The refrigerator runs more efficiently when the air can circulate properly, so don't create a pile up or blockage.

- Keep eggs in the carton they came home from the store in. They will stay fresher longer in the carton than if stored in the egg compartment in the refrigerator door. Always check the carton for broken and cracked eggs before you buy them. Don't eat an egg that is cracked.

- Put items you use infrequently, such as cocktail onions, in the back. Leftovers should be up front where you won't forget about them.

- Keep uncooked meat and chicken in their original package *and* in a plastic bag or on a tray. Never let meat or poultry drip onto anything else.

- Make sure to eat the older items first and keep a watch out for food that is past its expiration date. When in doubt about any food still being good or not, throw it away.

- Consider getting into the habit of washing and drying your fresh fruit and vegetables when you get home from the store. You may find it makes cooking a meal or grabbing a nutritious snack much easier if that chore is already done.

Freezer. The temperature in your freezer should be zero or less. Food needs to be frozen in a way that protects it from freezer burn or drying out. Use plastic freezer bags or plastic containers with lids that seal tightly. Unless it is properly labeled, avoid wrapping anything in aluminum foil as it becomes hard to recognize the item without unwrapping. Keep a permanent marker close to the freezer and make it a habit to label and date what you store. Frozen vegetables and packaged foods can be frozen in their original containers. Don't wait too long to eat what you have in the freezer. Again, eat the older items first.

Snacks. When you are living on your own you may be inclined not to want to cook. Have you heard the remark, "I don't like cooking just for myself?" If you let it, this notion is a direct path to snacking and little mini-meals (or frequent trips through your favorite drive-thru). While our bodies can handle reasonable amounts of junk food, be mindful to fill your home with healthy foods so you will not be having donuts, chips, ice cream, and soda for your dinner. Make it a point not to have high-fat, low-nutrition items sitting around your place to fill up on instead of eating something that's better for you. Enjoy those treats when you visit your friends!

Snack List. This list may remind you of snack time in kindergarten.

- Dried fruit
- Fresh fruit
- Granola
- Trail mix
- Nuts
- Popcorn
- Raisins
- Rice cakes
- Juice
- Yogurt, low fat

Water. Don't underestimate the value of good plain water. Drink lots of it. Constantly buying bottled water can be expensive, so try to buy a water purifier or filter as soon as you can afford it. Remember never to use hot tap water for cooking or drinking. Hot water may contain impurities from the water heater. Also, never drink chlorinated water.

Buying only organic food might be out of your reach right now. The Environment Working Group (*www.ewg.org/foodnews*) offers recommendations on which produce you should try to always buy organic and which have the least risk of exposure to pesticides. Here are some of their suggestions:

Try to Buy Organic	Lesser Risk Conventional Produce
Celery	Onions
Peaches	Avocados
Strawberries	Sweet Corn
Apples	Pineapples
Blueberries (Domestic)	Mangos
Nectarines	Sweet Peas
Sweet Bell Peppers	Asparagus
Spinach	Kiwi
Collard Greens/Kale	Cabbage
Cherries	Eggplant
Potatoes	Cantaloupe (Domestic)
Grapes (Imported)	Watermelon

Food Safety. The U.S. Department of Agriculture, Food Safety and Inspection Service offers educational information on many food safety topics. The web address is *www.fsis.usda.gov.*

You should know how to handle and prepare food safely not only to protect yourself from foodborne illness, but also to protect anyone you may cook for, especially children or the elderly. Foodborne illness can be dangerous and knowing how to handle and prepare food correctly is critical.

- Shop for perishable items last, come straight home, and put them in the refrigerator or freezer.

- Items that are most likely to contain bacteria, such as meat, poultry, and seafood, should not be allowed to drip on other items in the refrigerator. Also, their packaging materials can cause crosscontamination.

- Wash your hands before you start cooking anything and after you handle raw meat, poultry, seafood, or eggs. Every time.

- Always clean kitchen surfaces with kitchen disinfectant or hot, soapy water, before, during, and after food preparation.

- Cooked food should not be handled with the same utensils that you used with raw food unless you have carefully washed them first. Wash anything that raw meat and poultry touch before you use it again.

- There are three safe ways to defrost frozen food. The refrigerator method requires you to put the frozen item in the refrigerator to bring it up from 0 degrees to 40 degrees. This will take at least a day. Cold water thawing is putting the food in a leak-proof plastic bag and submerging it in *cold* tap water. You have to change the water every 30 minutes until the food is thawed. A pound will take about an hour. The last method is defrosting in the microwave. Food defrosted in the microwave must be cooked as soon as it is thawed because some parts of it may have already become warm and reached the best temperature for bacteria to grow.

None of the safe defrosting methods involve taking food from the freezer and laying it on the counter until it is ready to be cooked. The center of the food may be frozen, but the outer layer will rise above 40 degrees and bacteria will start to multiply.

- Ground meat needs to be cooked until the inside reaches at least 160 degrees. This means the inside should be brown.

- Never eat undercooked or rare poultry. The minimum internal temperature needs to reach 165 degrees.

- The lowest setting to safely roast poultry or meat is 325 degrees.

- Never eat raw eggs or foods that contain raw or partially cooked eggs.

- Don't eat perishable food that has been sitting out for more than two hours.

- Generally, put leftovers in the refrigerator immediately after your meal. However, putting anything hot into your refrigerator can raise the temperature of the refrigerator significantly, so wait until the food has cooled from hot to warm. Store food in shallow containers that allow the food to cool quickly and evenly.

- Use or throw away leftovers within four days.

- If you do not have a dishwasher, don't let your dirty dishes sit in water for a long time. The condition is just right for bacteria to grow. Rinse and stack if you want, but ideally all dirty dishes should be washed within two hours.

Dining Out

Some of us would rather eat at our favorite restaurant than cook. Yet, when you are just starting out on your own, dining out may not be practical. It certainly can be expensive. If you have limited resources yet still want to eat out occasionally, here are a few tips that may help:

- Check the paper for discount coupons. New restaurants often offer discounts to entice people to visit. The city where you live may have brochures for tourists that you can pick up free at the grocery store, library, and so on. These pamphlets are usually full of discount or "buy one, get one free" dining coupons.

- Lunch prices are usually less than dinner prices. Treat yourself to a big lunch and make yourself a light dinner.

- Avoid ordering drinks of any kind. Sticking with water will help keep your check total low.

- Share an entree with a friend and split the cost. This only works in restaurants that allow it and do not impose a per person charge.

- Don't worry if you are not financially able to eat at the restaurant you really want to try right now. You eventually will. If eating out means you must limit where you can visit, then that's the way it has to be, and good for you that you are not living beyond your means.

Dining Skills. Ideally we should all have only one set of dining skills that we use both in public and in private. Unfortunately, this is not the norm. People tend to be much more lax about the way they eat at home, alone, and with family, than when they eat out in public. The downside to this approach is that when they are out in public, it's much harder to use the correct skills because the skills are not automatic; the skills are rusty or nonexistent, and the person ends up feeling awkward. This is all easily avoided by learning basic dining skills and incorporating the skills into daily life until they become a well-developed habit.

Buy *The Little Book of Etiquette* by Dorothea Johnson. The tiny book has all the correct and current information you need to know to become a savvy diner.

Napkin. The napkin has two functions. Its first use is to just sit unfolded in your lap and catch any drips or spills. Secondly, it is used to discreetly dab the corners of your mouth. It is not used to do major wiping of any other part of your face, particularly your nose. Carry a facial tissue with you or a handkerchief, but do not use your napkin to wipe or blow your nose. It is also not used to wipe crumbs off the table. Put your napkin on the seat of your chair if you temporarily leave the table during the meal and leave it directly in front of you when you leave the restaurant. If your plate is still there, leave your napkin to the left of the plate.

Posture. Yes, you should sit up straight and keep your elbows off the table. Unless you eat Continental-style, where it is appropriate to rest both wrists on the table edge, you should keep your arm and forearm off the table as well.

Silverware. This is an area of dining that a lot of people struggle with. It is the area that most reveals how much dining knowledge you possess.

- Do not worry too much about which piece of silverware to use. The outside pieces are used first. The pieces should be removed after every course, so you will easily figure out which piece to use next. If you see a fork and a spoon lying horizontally above the plate, they are to be used with your dessert.

- There is only one correct way to hold your silverware when cutting your food. It does not involve holding the knife or fork in your fists and sawing at your plate. Hold the knife in your right hand, blade turned down toward the plate. Put the tip of your index finger on the blade, where it meets the handle. Hold the handle with your thumb and middle finger about two inches away from the blade. These fingers hold the knife while the pressure from your index finger forces the blade to cut. Hold your fork in your left hand with the tines facing down. Put your left index finger on the center of the base of the tines. Your thumb should be below the handle, while your other fingers are curled around the bottom part of the handle. Cut with a forward stroking motion toward your body.

- If, after cutting, you secure a piece of food on the tines and directly bring the fork to your mouth with your left hand (tines still down), you are eating Continental-style. The knife stays in your right hand. This is the easiest, quietest, and most graceful style of eating. If you put your knife down and change the fork from left hand to right, you are eating American-style. As the name implies, it is mostly only Americans who eat this way.

- Although it is very common for diners to prop their silverware up against their plate with half of it resting on the table, it is not correct. The rule is—once you pick up a piece of silverware, it should never rest on the table again.

Rest your knife and fork over your plate when you are paused during your meal. Your knife should be on the right, pointed to about ten o'clock on your plate and the blade should face inward. The fork tines should be turned down, cross the knife blade and face about two o'clock on your plate. They can extend over the plate about an inch, but do not rest them on the table.

- When you have finished eating, put both pieces of silverware side by side on the right side of your plate. The knife should be on the outside with the blade facing the fork.

- Do not leave your spoon in your soup bowl, cup, mug, or sorbet dish when you have finished. Place it on the underlying plate.

- Don't be overly concerned if you drop a piece of silverware. You should not get up from your chair to pick it up unless it is lying where it could cause someone to trip. Just signal to the server. The server will get you a replacement and also pick up the dropped piece.

Offensive Behavior. You can easily guard against being unintentionally offensive at the table by keeping a few things in mind:

- When dining out, treat the wait staff with courtesy and respect. Remember to use the words "please" and "thank you" every now and then.

- Resist the urge to blow on any hot food.

- Make sure your mouth is completely closed while chewing and never, ever talk with food in your mouth.

- Avoid fiddling with your hair or scratching your head at the table. Never comb or brush your hair in a dining area.

- Don't stretch to reach something across someone's place setting. Ask the person to pass it.

- Keep your fingers away from your mouth. Use a toothpick in the rest room to remove food stuck in your teeth. Toothpicks should not be used anywhere near the table, or while leaving the restaurant.

- Watch your vocabulary at the table. Some things that should never be discussed during a meal are body functions, illness, diets, food preferences, and anything else that might offend someone.

Restaurants. When eating in a restaurant, remember to use all your dining skills and be familiar with the following:

- If you are the host or hostess (meaning you did the inviting) the responsibility of choosing where you are going to eat is yours. Sure, if you wish, you can say to your guest, "I'm thinking we'll go to 22nd Street Landing. How does that sound to you?," but try to avoid the conversation that goes:

"So, where do you want to eat?"
"I don't care. Where do you want to eat?"
"I don't care. Wherever you want."
"I don't know. What do you think?"

Does this sound familiar? It's very common for people to each pay their own way when they eat out and so the decision can be mutual, but if you are hosting don't be hesitant to take the lead.

- Try not to take the best seat at your table. The best seat is the one that has the best view of the restaurant. It should be given to your guest.

- Take off your baseball cap.

- Your personal items, such as keys, sunglasses, hats, and briefcases, do not belong on the table. A purse belongs on the floor near your feet, or if it is small, in your lap.

- If you sit down at a table that has a coffee cup already sitting there, do *not* turn it over to indicate that you do not want coffee. The server will ask you and if you decline, the server will remove the cup.

- When you have finished eating, leave your plate where it is. You shouldn't stack the dirty plates and push them to the edge of the table.

- Absolutely never withhold a tip because you are trying to economize! The average tip is between 15 and 20 percent of the total bill before taxes. If the service was really poor you may want to leave less; if the service was great feel free to leave more. Practice figuring out how to calculate tipping so you can determine the amount quickly. Don't get your dinner guest involved with discussing and calculating the tip.

Being a Dinner Guest. Remember not only to use your dining skills when you are invited to eat at a restaurant or in someone's home, but to keep in mind the following as well:

- When you are invited to dinner or to a party, make sure you respond in a timely fashion. Don't leave it up in the air as to whether you are coming or not.

- Unless you specifically have been invited to do so, never bring a guest with you.

- Never be late. If you know you will be more than ten or fifteen minutes late, call and let your host/hostess know. Also, it is not considerate to arrive early.

- As a dinner party guest, arrive bearing a gift – even if it's a very small one. Don't bring your host/hostess something that needs immediate attention, such as flowers that need to be put in water and arranged. If you dine with the host regularly it is not necessary to bring something every visit.

- Wait until your host or hostess picks up their napkin before you do.

- An invited guest is supposed to contribute something to the conversation. It is your responsibility to join in the conversation, yet to remember the things you should not talk about at the table. With those you do not know extremely well, you can pretty much add to the list of taboo subjects discussions about money, religion, and controversial matters of the day.

- Time the pacing of your eating to match the pace of others present. You shouldn't race to the finish or still be shoveling it in when everyone else is done.

- If the dinner was with someone you do not normally eat with (for example, not at your cousin's house where you regularly eat four nights a week), it is correct to send a thank you note.

For more free tips, resources and how-to information please visit *www.LifeSkills101.com.*

Related Reading

Dining Skills A to Z: A Practical Guide to Today's Table Manners and Dining Etiquette by Tina Pestalozzi. Stonewood Publications; 2014.

The Etiquette Advantage in Business: Personal Skills for Professional Success by Peggy Post and Peter Post. Harper Resource; 2005.

Emily Post's Etiquette by Peggy Post. Empire Books; 2012.

Everyday Food: Fresh Flavor Fast: 250 Easy, Delicious Recipes for Any Time of Day by Martha Stewart Living Magazine. Clarkson Potter; 2010.

Food Inc.: A Participant Guide: How Industrial Food is Making Us Sicker, Fatter, and Poorer-And What You Can Do About It by Participant Media and Karl Weber Public Affairs; 2009.

The Gorgeously Green Diet by Sophie Uliano. Plume; 2009.

The Healthy College Cookbook by Alexandra Nimetz , Jason Stanley, Emeline Starr and Rachel Holcomb. Storey Publishing, LLC; 2009.

How to Boil Water by Food Network Kitchens. Wiley; 2006.

How to Cook Everything The Basics: All You Need to Make Great Food -- With 1,000 Photos by Mark Bittman. Wiley; 2012.

The Natural Kitchen: Your Guide to the Sustainable Food Revolution (Process Self-Reliance Series) by Deborah Eden Tull. Process; 2010.

The Pleasures of Cooking for One by Judith Jones. Knopf; 2009.

Power Foods: 150 Delicious Recipes with the 38 Healthiest Ingredients by The Editors of Whole Living Magazine. Clarkson Potter; 2010.

The Ultimate Student Cookbook: From Chicken to Chili by Tiffany Goodall. Firefly Books; 2010.

Chapter 7

Becoming a Savvy Consumer

Consumer Know-How

You have been making choices about how to spend your money for many years. When you were younger, did you ever agonize over what to buy with the cash gift a relative gave you, when there were so many things you wanted? You did your best with the money you had and you learned some money management skills along the way. Well, now is the time to kick those skills into high gear. From here on out you've got to make the best decisions you possibly can to become a sharp and savvy **consumer.**

If you are young and just starting out, your income is not anywhere near what it will be in the future. Most likely your resources are limited, and your life is highly impacted by each financial choice you make. Yet, the need to be a savvy consumer does not disappear when you have greater resources. Later, you will make frequent decisions on more expensive expenditures. Regardless of your income, make it a point to be an intelligent and well-informed consumer.

Prioritize. Once you formulate what your goals are, you must prioritize your expenditures. For example, if your primary desire is to live on your own, obviously you are deciding that a top priority is to spend money for housing. You can decide if having one or more roommates is an option for you. Not everyone is cut out for sharing their living quarters, and you must make the decision that is right for you. You may decide that your housing costs are a higher priority than the year and model of the car you drive. The idea here is that your choices must meet your needs and you must finance those choices in the wisest possible way.

This brings us to the bottom line when it comes to consumer spending. Is what you're spending your money on something you really need, or only want, and is it a wise choice?

Before You Buy

Ask yourself these questions before you allow your money to flow away from you:

- Am I purchasing something I really need?
- Does the item or service itself meet and fit my needs?
- Do I need to do any research before I buy?
- Have I done enough comparison shopping to make the purchase?
- Do I feel pressured to make this purchase?
- Can I truly afford this?
- Is there additional cost involved in this purchase?
- What's the worst thing that will happen if I don't buy this today?

Needs versus Wants. It's sometimes a pretty fuzzy line that separates your needs from your wants. Sure you want premium channel cable TV, but do you need it? These are the kinds of choices you are going to be up against. When you think about it, most of our purchases are for things we want all right, but not necessarily for goods and services that our survival or well-being depends upon. It's amazing how much we can do without if we have to. I don't want anyone to go without what he or she needs, but sometimes the habit of suspending our desires for *things* and *stuff,* until a better time, is the only practical option to exercise. Waiting may not be easy, but for some people, it certainly may be necessary.

Fitting the Need. On the surface a purchase may be just what you think you need, yet deeper examination proves that it doesn't exactly fit. For example, the cost of the used car you found may be just what you want to pay. It's in pretty good shape, but wait . . . what's this? It gets very, very poor gas mileage and your commute to work is forty-five miles each way! If you plan on driving the car to work, it would be in your best interest to keep looking.

You do not ever want to be sorry that you bought something you did. An example of this would be buying a desperately-needed winter coat only to realize the fabric should not be worn in the rain or snow, which is what you needed it for, and that it is dry-clean-only and will cost a mini-fortune to keep clean. Everyone has made thoughtless purchases at one time or another. Take the time to completely think through each purchase, and you'll find that your bad buys are few and far between.

Research. Today, we are fortunate to be able to take advantage of a tremendous amount of consumer research information. We have the benefit of consumer buying guides and consumer advocacy groups. There is information out there somewhere on just about every purchase you can think of making. Go to your local library or book store. Research online. For major purchases, check with the manufacture of the product you are considering to gain the knowledge you need to be able to compare it to similar products. There is an old saying: "Buyer beware." It's your responsibility to be aware of what you're buying.

Compare. Think about comparison shopping not only regarding the price of the product or service, but also with regard to the features of an item. For example, some small appliances have additional features for the same price of other models that do not.

Shopping around to get the best price is usually always worth it. Yet, keep in mind that the savings does have to be "worth it." By this I mean, it is not worth driving all over town the entire afternoon to save one or two dollars. First of all, your time is valuable and second, you are using up gas and incurring wear on your car. Not to mention that you will probably get hungry, go to a drive thru, and spend the few dollars you may have saved.

Don't forget that when you have decided on an exact item, you can call a store and ask the price for the item you want. This makes it easy to find the lowest possible price. Also check the paper for advertisements. This works especially well for seasonal items. Often you will spot the same item advertised at one store offered for less somewhere else.

Pressure. Pressure to make a purchase can come at you from several directions, not just from a salesperson who may be earning a commission and needs to make a sale. You may have time constraints. You may decide "just to get it," because it will be easier than thinking about it some more, shopping around some more, and returning back to the store again. You may have put off making a purchase for an upcoming event and now the pressure is on to buy something, anything close to what you need.

While operating under pressure in some circumstances may be appropriate, it is difficult to make the best consumer choices when you are under the gun. Resist feeling pressured into making a purchase that is not exactly what you need or can afford. If you do, learn from your mistakes and do what it takes; for example, planning ahead next time; to avoid the same situation in the future.

Remember all the talk of peer pressure in school? Well, for some people it never seems to go away, although it may change its form. Have you ever felt you wanted something because someone else had it? Don't get started in the "who has the most toys" game. It's a long trip to nowhere.

When I was in college I would rush to the bookstore at the start of every term to make sure I could pick a used textbook—at substantial savings. I had friends who would never buy a used textbook, with their big yellow stickers that didn't easily come off, because they felt it was a sign they didn't have money. I didn't care. I was not about to pressure myself into buying new when I was saving so much.

You may also be directly influenced by someone you know to buy something that *they* actually want. It's a good idea to ask for advice and information from friends and family before you make any major purchase. It's nice to run the idea by another person, perhaps hear something you haven't considered, or talk to someone who made a similar purchase in the past. Yet, keep in mind that the real user of the product or service is you, and your opinion is what ultimately should count the most. Do not let yourself be pressured or talked into buying something your gut feeling tells you is wrong for you, just because your best friend wants you to buy it. Trust yourself to figure out what is right for you.

Affordability. Are your finances going to be adversely affected in any way if you make this purchase? Can you make the purchase and still have funds left over to cover your other expenses? Do you have the cash? If you are putting a charge on your credit card, are you going to be able to pay the balance when your statement arrives or will you have to finance this purchase? Is this purchase worth incurring debt? Give yourself honest answers to these questions.

Additional Cost. It may not be a big deal if you need to buy batteries for the digital camera you just bought. It may be a bigger deal if you realize the old motorcycle you just bought will be needing tires soon and a new battery. How much is registration and insurance? Title fees? Storage fees in the winter because you do not have a garage and the living room isn't all that practical? You get the idea. Think about additional costs that might come up, such as how much is that hard to fix item going to cost to get repaired? Go for the low maintenance items and items that will not require extraordinary servicing.

Worst Case Scenario. This question is particularity helpful for the times when you are undecided or feeling pressured. Sure the item may not be there if you come back looking for it later. What then? Is the item so special that you would *truly* regret not having bought it? Most likely you could track it down somewhere else.

Is your need for the item so great that it will truly impact your life if you don't buy it today? Try to resist feeling like "I've got to buy this right now." Take your time and think through every purchase.

Big Ticket Items. There is a lot to think about when you buy anything, but especially when you make major purchases. In particular, make sure you do the necessary research and price comparisons. In addition to a traditional search, try the price-comparison search engine *www.pricegrabber.com.*
Learn when to buy quality goods. In some instances spending a few dollars more to purchase something well-made and long-lasting is the wisest way to go, that is, if the item is actually going to be genuinely useful to you. For instance, no matter how well made a dress may be, it won't be cost-effective if you only wear it once.

When you are just starting out, almost anything above the cost of food and shelter may seem like a major purchase. Anything over $500 is definitely a major expenditure. When you are satisfied that a major purchase, over $500, is right (you thought it through and did the necessary research and price comparisons), there is still one more thing you can do. You can haggle over the price. Nicely and firmly. You have nothing to lose and you may end up saving. Try it; you may be surprised.

> Keep a file that includes warranties, instruction manuals, and receipts for your purchases.

Hint. If you become tempted to rent furniture and/or appliances, carefully consider the idea. In certain circumstances, for instance, when you know you will need the items for only a very limited time, it may be a good idea to rent, but it generally is not to your advantage. Check the contract very carefully and make sure you know exactly what renting will actually cost.

After You Buy

It sounds really obvious, yet one of the smartest things you can do is take good care of the things you spend your hard earned money on. Take care of your clothes and you will need to replace them less frequently. Take good care of your car and you will decrease the chances of having to pour your cash into getting it repaired and yes, again, replacing it. Cars are now built better than ever and will last for many, many years with the right care. It only makes sense to want whatever you own to last as long as possible. You have probably already developed rules concerning your belongings. If you are someone who has been careless in the past with your possessions; for instance, loaning things to friends who never seem to return them; you may want to start practicing a little more care now that you have so many financial responsibilities. Replacing an item because of carelessness is not cost-effective and will take you further away from reaching your financial goals.

Extended Warranties. When you purchase certain items, such as appliances, electronics, and so forth, you might be asked to purchase an extended warranty. While you might think this is not a bad idea, keep in mind that extended warranties are not used most of the time. This means the chances are good that you will never use the coverage you are paying for. This coverage may make sense for are certain new technology items. Visit *www.consumerreports.org* for information to help you make the decision.

Buying Insurance

You've heard about insurance. You choose a policy, pay your **premium** (or payment for the coverage,) and hope you never need to file a claim. Auto insurance will probably be your first experience at purchasing insurance. It is only one of the many types of insurance you will need to acquire in your lifetime. You may need renter's insurance soon and home owner's insurance down the line. Whatever your needs are, this is one more area in which it is critical to do your homework.

Insurance is a big business. Always shop around for the best policy. This means the best coverage, with the lowest rate, on the benefits you are likely to use the most. The companies that issue insurance are rated by several agencies. Buy your policy from a company with a high rating. Again, do your research. Ask friends and relatives. Hop back on the Internet and try the free quote services. The following are a few types of insurance you will need to consider now or in the very near future:

Insurance

- Auto
- Renter's or Home Owner's
- Health
- Term Life

There are many large insurance companies that offer complete insurance coverage. This means you can obtain policies for different needs through the same company.

Auto. Auto coverage rates vary greatly from one company to another. Be sure to check with large national insurers. Buying direct without an insurance agent may save you money. The amount you pay for auto insurance will not only depend on the coverage you buy, but several other factors as well.

Your rates will be affected by the type of car you drive. If you have the hot car of the moment, your insurance rate will be higher. The type of vehicles that are most often stolen cost more to insure than others. Your age, sex, marital status, and driving record will be a consideration. Rates are usually more if you are under 25, a male, single, or worse, all three. Not having an accident or moving violation will help keep your rates low. The number of miles you normally drive are also a factor as well as whether or not you are a student.

While there are plenty of variables, one of the biggest factors is how high you set your **deductible.** (The amount you are required to pay before an insurance reimbursement is made.) A higher deductible will decrease your premium. Carefully consider how much coverage you actually need. Think about the assets you need to protect when calculating how much **liability insurance** to purchase. Make sure you have adequate coverage without being overinsured. Get quotes on several different coverage amounts, at different deductibles, before you decide.

Health. Hopefully, you already have health coverage in place, perhaps by being included in your parents' policy or by being covered in a student health plan. Perhaps you are fortunate enough to have a job that offers health benefits. However, if you do not yet have health insurance, you must find a way to get coverage as soon as you reasonably can. A good place to start is *www.HealthCare.gov*. This government site was created to give you a place to compare health insurance options, and provide tools to help you find the coverage that is appropriate for your situation. It is also the site to use to learn about the new health care law The Affordable Care Act and to access your state's Health Insurance Marketplace. Every health insurance plan in the new Marketplace will offer comprehensive coverage. You can compare all your insurance options based on price, benefits, quality, and other features that may be important to you. You'll be able to enroll yourself directly through the website. When key parts of the health care law take effect in 2014, you may be eligible for a free or low-cost plan, or a tax credit that lowers your monthly premiums right away.

When shopping for a policy, the first thing you'll look at is the premium. Yet, just as important as the premium cost, is how much you have to pay when you get services, and what exact services the plan covers—and leaves out. Often, there is a direct tradeoff between how much you pay for health insurance and the extent of the covered benefits. You want the best coverage that you can afford.

You'll need to examine the annual deductible, the amount you pay for services once you've paid the deductible, how much, if anything, is due at the time of service (this is known as a co-payment) and how much in total you will have to pay if you become ill (this is known as the out-of-pocket maximum).

In addition to traditional plans, there is also a High Deductable Health Plan. Here you have a high deductible, with a low premium, and can establish a medical saving account in which the funds are not subject to federal income tax at the time of deposit and can be withdrawn for medical expenses.

No matter which insurance agency issues your health plan, you must be responsible for reading and understanding the policy. Here again, don't assume anything and don't hesitate to ask questions.

- Be aware that short-term policies exist that will allow you to have coverage for up to six months. This may work for you until you can find an employer-sponsored health plan.

Renter's. You may think you do not have enough to insure, and in the very beginning you may be right. Yet, items add up quickly and soon you will accumulate enough to seriously consider renter's coverage. If you think it would cost close to $10,000 or more to replace what you have, it's time to purchase a renter's policy. Don't make the mistake of assuming your landlord's policy will cover your personal possessions. You need your own protection.

Understand what losses the policy covers. Typically, renter's insurance covers loss due to fire, smoke, theft, vandalism, and many other occurrences, but not losses due to earthquakes or flood, although you may be able to purchase the additional coverage with a **rider** or **floater** to your policy.

Renter's insurance involves personal property coverage and liability protection. If your guest gets hurt at your place and sues you for damages, your insurance covers your cost up to your **liability** limit.

You will need to make sure you understand the difference between a policy that pays **replacement cost** or **replacement value** and one that pays out **actual cash value.** If your old television is stolen, actual cash value coverage pays out what the insurance company determines the old television was worth, and chances are the amount will be nowhere near the amount needed to replace it. A policy that pays replacement cost will pay what it costs to purchase the item again. Keep in mind that renter's insurance also has a deductible. That is, you will receive the amount owed you minus your deductible, or if the amount owed to you is not more than the deductible, the policy does not pay out.

Make sure you thoroughly understand the details and conditions regarding the company's procedure in paying your claim. For example, will you have to buy replacement items with your funds and submit receipts before you get a reimbursement?

Also, make sure you research what the policy covers on items such as electronics, jewelry, art, and antiques, which may only be covered up to a certain amount. If you have any of these items, make sure you discuss this with the insurance company so that you will be buying the correct coverage for your belongings. You may need to purchase an additional rider for these articles. Remember the safe-deposit or strongbox suggestion from Chapter 2? Keep the receipts of all your major purchases as well as a photographic inventory of your belongings in the box. The receipts may be used as proof that you bought an item in question. It is to your advantage to be as prepared as possible in the event you ever need to file a claim. Photograph possessions as you acquire them or video the entire contents of your place. Keep an up-to-date running inventory of your belongings. In the event of a disaster the last thing you will want to do is try to recall every item you owned. Here again, be prepared.

Hint: There are certain things an insurance company will give a discount on. No matter what type of policy you are checking into, ask the representative what discounts the company offers. For instance, you may receive a discount on your renter's insurance if you have smoke alarms and fire extinguishers. You may receive a discount on your auto policy if your car has an alarm. Don't forget to ask.

It is probably premature to worry about life insurance and home owner's coverage now when there are so many other things to get in place. Yet, you should know this very basic information:

Life Insurance. This type of insurance protects those who depend on you from the loss of your financial support in the event of your death. If you are not yet responsible for the financial support of someone else, and you do not own property, you probably do yet not need this type of insurance.

Life insurance is not necessarily a permanent need. You may need heavy coverage when you have the responsibility of a family and lots of debt obligations. In your later years, being lightly insured or having no coverage at all may be appropriate if your financial estate is in place.

When it is time to shop for life insurance, I recommend you seriously consider only term life. With a term policy you are covered for a specific amount of time, for instance 10, 20 or even 30 years. Term life insurance is generally the most cost-effective type of policy for providing a benefit for your loved ones.

If you are ever attempted to buy a whole-life policy (one in which you are covered your whole life) or a cash value policy, I suggest you go back and do some more research. Make sure you are not depending solely on the information provided by the insurance company or agent for the company. Making whole-life sound like a terrific deal is the agent's job. Do independent research.

Home Owner's. Similar to renter's insurance in that it provides personal property and personal liability coverage, home owner's insurance also provides protection against damage to, or loss of, the dwelling you own. When you finance your first home, the lender might require you to purchase this type of coverage. Again you will need to do the research, decide how much coverage you need in order to have sufficient protection, and decide which, if any, additional riders to the policy you need to purchase.

Buying a Car

You will probably always remember your first car and the independence and freedom it represented. If you haven't made the purchase yet, here are a few things to think about.

Before You Buy. While you may have an idea as to the kind of car you would like, what is probably more important is to have a very clear idea as to the price you are going to be able to afford to pay for the car. If you will be seeking a loan from a bank or credit union, shop for the loan first and get preapproved before you become too far involved with selecting your car. The loan amount that you qualify for will influence the options available to you, as will the amount that you have available for a down payment.

When deciding how much you can afford, be sure to factor in all expenses related to the purchase, such as taxes, fees, and registration; and to consider the monthly expenses involved, such as the monthly interest cost, maintenance costs, and the insurance premium.

Promise yourself that you will stick to the limit that you have set. It's easy to drift off and start looking at more car than you can afford. Stay within your limit amount and do not let yourself be talked into anything else.

If you are buying a used car, compare the asking price to the average **Kelly Blue Book** price. (Visit *www.kbb.com* or your local library to find out.) And, whether you buy your car from a dealer or a private party, have the car inspected by an expert mechanic you can trust. Make sure you know exactly what you are getting into. Ask yourself the questions from the "Purchase Check List" mentioned earlier. Be especially sure the car is the right one for you. It may be a while before you buy another one.

Your Test Drive. Take every car that you are seriously considering for a good, objective test drive. This is where you will see how well suited the two of you are. Keep in mind that the car that is most visually appealing to you may, in fact, not be the one that is exactly right for you. So remember, the longer the test drive, the better.

Try to have the least possible distractions. Don't hesitate to tell the salesperson (if he or she insists on going with you) that you would like quiet so you can concentrate. Check the radio when you get back to the lot, not during the drive.

The test drive is very important because the information you gain is critical to the final success of your search. Here again, take your time and trust yourself to make the right choice.

- How is the visibility? Check out the blind spots.
- How does the steering feel? Are you comfortable with it?
- How well does the car accelerate? Try to find an on-ramp to test acceleration. How well does it accelerate with the air conditioner on?
- Try to find a rough road to see how well the car rides.
- How does the car perform in tough traffic?
- Try the reverse gear. Do all gears work smoothly?
- Do you understand the instrument panel? Is it easy to use and read?
- What is your gut reaction to the car?

Protecting Yourself

You are accepting a lot of responsibilities when you live on your own. You'll spend time learning how to handle your finances; you'll make sound decisions. Crimes of financial and identity fraud are real in our society. You need to be aware of this so you will use your best judgment and exercise caution in your personal and financial life. Part of being a savvy consumer is being aware of potential fraud in your virtual surroundings and taking the steps you can to avoid it.

- I wrote in Chapter 2 that you should use discretion with regard to your Social Security number. The same applies to your credit card numbers. Do not ever give out either numbers over the phone to a business or service provider *who has called you.* Make sure you know to whom you are talking. Even if you are given a number to call back, check with the phone company to make sure the number matches the business.

- Take time to look at the itemized charges on your credit card statement. Call the card company immediately if you think there has been an unauthorized charge to your account. Check your phone bills, also.

- If you feel you must always carry a credit card with you, only carry one. Do not routinely carry your Social Security card.

- If you have a personal identification number from your financial institution—do *keep it a secret!* Do not use the last four digits of your Social Security number, your birthday, your dog's name, and so on for the number and do not write it on anything you carry with you.

- Do not disclose personal information, such as your credit card number, Social Security number, mother's maiden name, and so forth in any e-mail message, unsecured Internet site, or over a wireless phone.

- Contact the Bureau of Motor Vehicles immediately if you think your driver's license number has been misused, for example, to write a bad check. You will need to get a new license and put a fraud alert on the old one.

- When you write a check to pay a bill by mail, drop the bill off at the post office or put it in a mail collection box. Never leave a check to be collected from your home mail box unless the box has a lock that can only be accessed by the postal carrier.

- Test the strength of every password you create at *www.passwordmeter.com.*

- Shred or completely destroy:

    ✓ All offers for credit cards you do not accept.

    ✓ Offers from your credit card company that include blank checks for balance transfers and cash advances.

    ✓ ATM receipts, after the transaction has been verified.

    ✓ Utility bills, pay stubs and canceled checks, etc. that are no longer needed for tax purposes or any other reason.

    ✓ All outdated papers containing your date of birth, Social Security number, user names and/ or passwords

- *Never* sign a blank or incomplete check, blank contract, or blank sheet of paper!

- Make it a habit to access a free copy of your credit report from *www.AnnualCreditReport.com.* You can order a free copy once a year from each of the three major consumer credit reporting companies, through the web site, mail or phone. Checking regularly will help you spot and deal with any suspicious items in a timely fashion.

- Most importantly—Trust your instincts. If your intuition tells you something is amiss, you may be right. While you do not need to live in fear of being a victim of financial or identity fraud, you will feel more empowered knowing you are taking steps to protect yourself.

The Federal Trade Commission's Identity Theft Helpline is *877.438.4338 (www.ftc.gov/idtheft).*

If you have reason to believe that you have been the victim of fraud or identity theft, contact the credit bureaus at:

Equifax:	*800.525.6285*
Experian:	*888.397.3742*
Trans Union:	*800.680.7289*

Reminder. Whether you're chatting in the checkout line with the person behind you, or posting on your favorite social network, be discerning about how much, and what, information you give out. For example, just because you're buying a lot of frozen food doesn't mean you should be chatting about living alone without anyone else at home to cook with. And just because you are having a great vacation, your posts don't need to tell everyone your house and its contents are available for the taking. Don't live your life being afraid and become overcautious, not speaking to strangers, for example—just operate with awareness.

Tipping

Somewhere along the line we learn that certain services performed for us by others require our tipping. While tipping in the United States is still voluntary for most services, it has become the expected and correct thing to do.

Learn which services require tipping and the correct amount to give. The accepted amounts vary, depending on the area of the country where you live. It is appropriate to tip in accordance with the service provided. For example, if the valet ran through wind and rain to bring your car to the door for you, consider adjusting the tip upward, while if the wait staff neglected you and provided poor service, you are free to adjust the tip accordingly.

Here are some general tipping expectations:

- Baggage Handlers: $1 and up per bag
- Barbers: 15%
- Bartender: $1 per drink. 50¢ for soft drink
- Beauty Operator: 10% to 20%
- Carwash Attendant: $1–$5
- Coat Check: $1 per coat
  $2 more for additional items
- Concierge: $5–$10 for getting you
  tickets or reservations
- Food Delivery Person: $2 for regular size order,
  $5 for large order
- Golf Caddy: 15% to 20% of green fees
- Hotel Housekeeper: $3 to $10 per day
- Manicurist / Pedicurist: 10% to 20%
- Masseuse: 10% to 20%
- Parking Attendant: $2 to $3 for bringing your
  car to you
- Pet Groomer   15%
- Room Service $5 if gratuity has not already
  been added to your check.
- Shampoo Person $2
- Shoe Shiner $2– $3
- Sommelier or Wine Steward: 15% of the cost of the bottle
- Tattoo or Piercing Artists: 10%–20%
- Taxi Drivers: 15% of the fare,
  $1–$2 extra for help with
  your bags
- Tow Truck Driver: $5
- Wait Staff: 15% to 20% of the total
  check before taxes

$ **Watching Your Pennies** $

*These suggestions count toward going green. Not only will they save you money, they are environmentally conscientious choices, as well.

- If you are going shopping just for the fun of it, leave your money, checkbook and credit cards at home.
- Don't shop when you are feeling any mood extremes. Being too tired, sad, or even too happy may cause you to make an unwise purchase.
- Buy used. Not junk, but used items that still have plenty of life left in them. Be careful; going to garage sales and flea markets can become addicting. *
- Check out your nearest beauty school. It may offer great savings not only on haircuts and nails, but also on spa services.
- If you or someone you know has a truck, pick up that new large purchase yourself and save delivery costs.
- Take full advantage of your local library for free use of movies, music, the Internet, newspapers, magazines and special events. *
- Set an amount limit on every gift you purchase and stick to it. If you give gifts during the holidays, try to spread your shopping throughout the entire year to avoid needing a large sum of money all at once.
- Give services, such as watching kids, lawn mowing, etc., instead of giving gifts. Write a heartfelt letter (a real one – on paper) instead of buying greeting cards. *
- Shop around before selecting a wireless phone. Compare prices and plans of several dealers and service providers to find the plan and the phone that best suit your needs. Think about the calls you typically make and the most cost effective way to meet your needs. Make sure you understand the terms and conditions of the contract, as you may be charged a heavy cancellation fee if you decide the plan isn't working for you.

- Buying food items from a vending machine costs at least twice as much as buying them in the grocery store.

- Wrap up your own coins, don't use change machines. The fee for the convenience of the machine usually runs about 8%. Get the wrappers from your bank for free.

- If you drink soda, save money by buying it in 2 liter bottles instead of in cans or at the convenience store.

- Try selling or trading items you no longer need on *on www.craigslist.com or www.ebay.com.* *

- Wash and then reuse plastic storage and freezer bags. *

- When considering buying any item of significant cost, be sure to ask if the item will be going on sale in the near future.

- If your doctor prescribes you a medication ask if he has any samples available.

- Whether it's with your credit card terms, phone, cable TV, or Internet services, always be careful when signing up for special or promotional rates. Be sure you know what the nonpromotional rate will be at the end of the initial period.

$ Your Clothes $

- Avoid trendy fashions. This may be the last thing you want to hear, but buying something that is going to be out of date within six months is definitely not cost-effective. Stick to the classics.

- Buy on sale. Don't pay retail. Clothes do not set too long on the racks before being marked down.

- Make sure a retail outlet store is a true outlet and that the clothes really are cheaper.

- Try to find a consignment shop in your area. Often there are bargains to be had on clothes that are still in style and good shape. *

- Avoid items that are "Dry Clean Only."

- There are several products available to help freshen and remove wrinkles from your "Dry Clean Only" garments. Using one may stretch out your trips to the cleaners.

- Buy items that can be worn with what you already have or that match other separates you buy. For example: Don't buy a top if it matches only one pair of pants.

- Consider taking a part-time job at a retail store that offers its employees a generous discount.

$ Your Car $

- Keep your driving record clean. Violations are expensive and your insurance rates will go up since you won't qualify for discounts.

- The most expensive time to buy a car from a dealer is March through June. Lots of people plan their summer vacations and purchase new cars. The weeks before Christmas and the first months of the new year are better times to negotiate a deal.

- Buying a preowned "new" car can save you thousands. Find one with 5,000 miles or less, that was a demo or rental.

- Here are a few ways you can save money on gas:

  ✓ Find the cheapest gas that is closest to your home by using the *Gas Prices* feature at *www.mapquest.com* or by checking *www.fuelmeup.com*. If the lowest price isn't close, make sure that the drive will be worth what you save.

  ✓ Keep your tires inflated to the correct pressure. Check them every week.

  ✓ Anticipate stop signs and lights and try to drive at a constant speed.

✓ Avoid hard braking as well as quick acceleration.

✓ When there's a line at the drive-thru, park and walk in.

✓ Share rides, consolidate errands, and walk or bike whenever possible.

$ Your Insurance $

• Shop around and around!!

• Find out what conditions qualify you for a discount.

• The higher the deductible, the lower the rates.

• Buying two or more policies from the same place may save you money, but only if it is insurance you were going to buy anyway.

Resources to contact for information and help:

Consumer World: *www.consumerworld.org*
A non-commercial guide to consumer resources.

Disability Information: *www.disability.gov*
Online resource for Americans with disabilities

Federal Citizen Information Center:
Help with consumer questions and problems:
www.consumeraction.gov
Government publications: *www.pueblo.gsa.gov*

Federal Communications Commission: *888.225.5322*
or *www.fcc.gov/cgb* Help information for telecommunications consumers.

Federal Reserve Board: Consumer Information:
www.federalreserve.gov/consumers.htm

Insurance Information Institute: *www.iii.org*
Information to help consumers understand insurance and how it works.

National Consumers League: *www.nclnet.org*
The Nation's oldest consumer organization.

National Geographic's *www.thegreenguide.com*
    Great information on the many ways you can play a
    part in helping the environment.

Privacy Rights Clearinghouse: *www.privacyrights.org*
    Nonprofit Consumer Information and Advocacy Orga-
    nization

U.S. Department of Health & Human Services:
    www.healthfinder.gov
    Guide to health information

For comparison quotes on insurance policies:
    Insurance Quote Services:

iQuote	*www.iquote.com*	*800.352.9742*
Net Quote	*www.netquote.com*	
Quote Smith:	*www.insure.com*	*855.430.7748*
Select Quote:	*www.selectquote.com*	*800.670.3213*

For more free tips, resources and how-to information please
visit *www.LifeSkills101.com.*

Related Reading:

To learn more about what you can do to protect your
identity, check out the book *50 Ways to Protect Your Identity in a Digital Age: New Financial Threats You Need
to Know and How to Avoid Them* by Steve Weisman. FT
Press; 2012.

Chapter 8

Staying Connected

Positive Actions

I believe everyone should live alone for awhile before they take on the additional responsibilities of a life partner or starting a family. Living alone gives you the time to discover who you really are and how you truly want to spend your life. It's having your place in the sun. Yet, I have known many young people who, even though they had looked forward to living on their own, have ended up not enjoying the experience to its fullest. We are not all cut out to live alone, but the experience can give invaluable insight. It can be a time of great personal discovery and growth, and best of all—fun!

I think one of the contributing factors to how successful you feel about living on your own is how well you are able to feel engaged in, and connected to, life itself. Living on your own is *not* similar to solitary confinement. It's a wonderful opportunity to challenge yourself to expand and explore all the riches of our world and to make a productive contribution to society. Having your own place may mean that for the first time in your life, you are able to have the social life you want or to pursue areas of interest you have always wanted to try. It could be that for the first time in your life, you are free to truly express who you really are and what you are all about.

A pitfall of living on your own is that you can easily begin to feel lonely. Unfortunately, many jobs today also contribute to the feelings of loneliness and isolation. Some people spend the entire working day alone at a computer terminal. It can take an enormous amount of energy and willpower to combat the negative feeling of loneliness, yet you must make the effort.

Build a life for yourself that is comfortable, interesting, and productive and your experience with living on your own will be positive. I hope the following suggestions are helpful:

Create a Comfortable Home. Even if you think you live in a "dump," do whatever you can to make your *home* as physically and emotionally comfortable as possible. You have your own style—express it! Turn your place into an environment where you look forward to spending time and one that works for you. If you want to leave an ongoing project out so you can work on it whenever you feel like it—now is your chance. If you want a drum set, amplifiers, and sound equipment in the living room instead of furniture, it's your choice. You are a grown-up now and can live the way you please.

Make the effort to create surroundings that make you feel like you are home. Buy a plant. (A philodendron is hardy and will tolerate mild neglect.) Put out pictures of people you love. Unpack any boxes that are still sitting around since you moved in. The more you can do to make your home feel like home—a place you enjoy being—the better off you will feel.

Family and Friends. Not everyone chooses to be connected to his or her family, and very often today, families are spread out across the country. If you do not have close family ties, the relationships that you cultivate with friends and coworkers become that much more important. As you know by now, friendships do require a certain amount of cultivation and effort. Being a good friend does require your time and awareness, but having a good friend is a priceless experience.

You've heard the expression, "You can never have too many friends." Friends can enhance your life beyond measure. Don't limit yourself just to people whom you already know. Seek out friends from all areas of your life. Young or old—from your job, school, or where you do volunteer work. We tend to gravitate toward people we feel comfortable around and who we feel are like us and share the same interests. Yet, I hope you also cultivate relationships with those who are different from you. Everyone has something unique to offer.

- Always use sound judgment and trust your instincts when it comes to the people you include in your life. Remember a true friend is respectful of you. Someone who asks you to compromise your integrity or break the law is someone you should not include in your life.

- Learn the skills involved in dealing with difficult people. You may have to face someone at work or at school who is hard to get along with. Turning a strained relationship with an acquaintance into a friendship may be too much of a reach, but having the skills to handle a difficult person without causing yourself undue stress can be a true blessing.

- Sooner or later you will find yourself being host or hostess to family and friends. With all entertaining, it is important to make your guests feel comfortable, but especially so when you have houseguests:

  ✓ Clean your home.

  ✓ Make room for your guests ahead of time. Clear an area where they can put their things. Make sure there is also space cleared in the bathroom to lay out items.

  ✓ Lay out clean towels and show your guests where they are located.

  ✓ Make sure your guests have enough bedding, and so forth.

  ✓ Have food available and ready.

  ✓ Anticipate your guests' needs and do your very best to make them feel at home.

Enrichment Classes. Taking a class just for the heck of it may be the last thing you think you want to do right now, but I encourage you to take every enrichment class that interests you or that you think you could benefit from. I have mentioned several subjects in this book that I think would be to your advantage to pursue and learn more about:

- *Basic Real Estate:* Learn as much as you can about buying and financing a home, so that when it comes time to purchase your own home, you will be a savvy buyer.

- *Car Maintenance:* Know how to handle routine tasks yourself as well as how to change a tire and jump-start your car.

- *Cooking:* A cooking class can be great fun and you (and your guests) can immediately reap the rewards of your learning a few different dishes.

- *Dance:* Be sure to learn the basic social dances.

- *Dealing with People:* Yes, there are even classes on dealing with difficult people.

- *Dining and Etiquette Skills:* Do not underestimate the importance of knowing the correct way to handle yourself in public, particularly if your career is one in which you are dealing directly with people.

- *Disaster Preparedness:* Learn how to be ready and how to deal with the types of disasters most common in your geographic area.

- *Exercise:* If taking an organized class is the only way you can get yourself to exercise, sign up! (If you are pursuing a business career, make sure you know how to play golf and tennis!)

- *Foreign Language:* Learn the language of a place you hope to someday visit and master any languages you now know.

- *Gardening:* Save money, create beauty and get great exercise by learning how to make your garden grow.

- *Money Management:* Understanding the best ways to handle not only your day-to-day money decisions, but the different ways to invest safely and wisely, is a valuable addition to your financial knowledge.

- *Public Speaking:* Taking a speech class or attending Toastmasters International will help build your public communication skills.

- *Relaxation:* Consider massage, meditation, and stress reduction.

- *Résumé Writing:* Learn how to write the résumé that is best for you and keep it current.

- *Self-Defense:* Learning the basics will help you feel more confident.

- *Taxes:* Obtain tips and advice and learn the tax laws so you can manage your money accordingly.

- *Time Management:* The more demands you have on your time, the more you need this knowledge.

- Being certified in the following areas is something that a potential employer may look at favorably:

   ✓ American Sign Language
   ✓ CPR
   ✓ First Aid, including the Heimlich Maneuver.

Look for classes at adult education facilities, community and civic centers, churches, YMCA's, and so forth. Many bookstores, libraries and cafes offer interesting classes free of charge. Our world is huge and brimming over with things to learn, and the returns of learning are enormous.

Volunteer. You are a unique individual and your community needs your contributions. Seek out ways to help others. If you had to do volunteer work or community service in high school, keep up the practice of offering your time to worthy causes and organizations. Not only does the organization that you help benefit from your time and effort, but few things are as personally rewarding as serving others.

www.allforgood.org	*www.nationalservice.gov*
www.servenet.org	*www.volunteermatch.org*

> If you think you don't have time to do volunteer work, perhaps you will consider being a blood donor. This does not take a lot of time but is an extremely important way to help others. Call your local chapter of the American Red Cross for information.

Organizations and Clubs. If you have a particular area of interest, chances are good that there is a club or organization of people in your area who also share your enthusiasm. For example, if you love to go canoeing, joining a canoe team may be just what you need; not only to enjoy the sport, but also to stay connected with others.

Don't hesitate to try different clubs and groups. If you find something just isn't working for you, you can move on to something else. The point is to stay engaged in an active life and not to fall into the isolation of being alone.

Hint: Organizations, clubs, and communities often sponsor free events. Attending community events, activities, and concerts is a great way to economize on your entertainment expenses, meet a variety of people, and stay in touch with what is going on in your area.

Worship. Some people know that organized worship is not for for them, while others instinctively know they need the fellowship experience that organized worship offers. If you are open to the idea of organized worship but have not yet found a place to attend that feels right to you, please keep looking until you do. Be open. Search for the place where you feel comfortable and spiritually nourished. Not only will positive fellowship enrich your life, but having a spiritual "family" can also give you the support base you may need.

Getting Help

When I started a small business, I was stunned at how many people went out of their way to offer help and assistance to make my business work. What surprised me the most was that other business people, people whom I had never met before, were offering me their expertise, lending me a hand, and doing what they could to help me get going. I will never forget their support.

My daughter had leukemia when she was nine years old. The disease caused her sternum to break, and caused several fractures in her back. For a while, she was unable to walk and had to be carried everywhere. Her low blood count made it impossible for her to be in public places. I couldn't leave her alone, and I couldn't take her anywhere except to her treatments. I was a single mother alone with all my family far away. A simple thing like getting to the store to buy food all of a sudden was a problem. I started to worry about how we were ever going to manage, but before I knew it, help arrived from the most *unexpected* people. I am telling you this because I want you to be sure you know and understand, that there are good, wonderful people in this world who love the opportunity to care for and help others who genuinely need a hand.

Don't ever feel too proud or embarrassed to ask someone for help. You can benefit greatly from other people's knowledge and life experience. Most people are flattered when asked to give an opinion or helpful advice. No one gets though life without the help of others, and we are all blessed when we are able to help each other.

A Final Word

Leaving your family home and moving out on your own is an important rite of passage. I hope it is a joyful, rewarding, and exciting time for you. You have the knowledge to make it a successful experience. You've been preparing for a long time . . . ever since you first heard the basics:

- Be nice.
- Pay attention.
- Wash up.
- Clean your room.
- Eat!
- Be careful.
- Go out and play!

You have my warmest wishes.

Related Reading

Better Than Good: Creating a Life You Can't Wait to Live by Zig Ziglar. Thomas Nelson; 2007.

The Civility Solution by P. M. Forni. St. Martin's Griffin; 2009.

The Complete Guide to the Gap Year: The Best Things to Do Between High School and College by Kristin M. White. Jossey-Bass; 2009.

Ecothrifty: Cheaper, Greener Choices for a Happier, Healthier Life by Deborah Niemann. New Society Publishers; 2012.

How to Build a Fire: And Other Handy Things Your Grandfather Knew by Erin Bried. Ballantine Books; 2010.

How to Sew a Button: And Other Nifty Things Your Grandmother Knew by Erin Bried. Ballantine Books; 2009.

Make Today Count: The Secret of Your Success Is Determined by Your Daily Agenda by John C. Maxwell. Center Street; 2008.

No Excuses!: The Power of Self-Discipline by Brian Tracy. Vanguard Press; 2011.

Personal Development for Smart People: The Conscious Pursuit of Personal Growth by Steve Pavlina. Hay House; 2009.

The 7 Habits of Highly Effective People by Stephen R. Covey. Free Press; 2004.

Ten Ways to Change the World in Your Twenties by Libuse Binder. Sourcebooks, Inc.; 2009.

The Thinking Life: How to Thrive in the Age of Distraction by P. M. Forni. St. Martin's Griffin; 2011.

Tuesdays with Morrie: An Old Man, a Young Man and Life's Greatest Lesson by Mitch Albom. Time Warner Paperbacks; 2003.

Wellbeing: The Five Essential Elements by Tom Rath and James K. Harter. Gallup Press; 2010.

Glossary

Actual cash value: The current depreciated value of an item, usually less than what it costs to replace it.

Consumer: One who buys or uses a product or service.

Credit bureaus: Private agencies that collect information about an individual's credit worthiness and sell that information to authorized users, such as banks and credit card companies.

Credit report or credit rating: A formal record and evaluation of an individual's or business's history of credit responsibility.

Debit: The accounting of a debt. For example, to debit an amount from your account is to deduct that amount.

Deductible: Under your insurance policy, the amount that you must pay before the insurance company begins paying on your claim.

Deductions: The expenses or items used to offset the amount of gross income or adjusted gross income on a tax return.

Dividends: Payment of a share of the earnings or profits of a corporation to shareholders.

Entropy: Lack of pattern or organization; disorder

Full faith and credit: The unconditional commitment to pay interest and principle on a debt; for example, a federal, state, or local government's pledge.

Golden Rule: That you should treat others according to how you would like them to treat you. Likewise, you should not treat others in ways that you would not like to be treated.

Gross income: Your total income, excluding amounts not subject to tax. Amount before deductions are made.

Hold: When a financial institution does not immediately credit all or part of a deposit.

Interest: Money charged for the use of borrowing money or money paid for the use of money.

Kelly Blue Book: A guide to car prices that can be found at most libraries, credit unions and banks or online at *www.kbb.com*.

Liability: Money that you owe.

Liability insurance: Coverage to protect against claims of injury or damage to other people or their property.

Lien: A legal right to take another's property to satisfy a debt.

Networking: Being involved with an association of individuals who may have common interests or provide mutual assistance, such as the sharing of information or services.

Overdraft protection: Coverage that allows you to draw in excess of your account balance.

Period or statue of limitations: Law that states the time within which legal proceedings must be started. Period of time the Internal Revenue Service can assess additional tax, or in which you can amend or change your tax return.

Precedence: Priority of order based on rank or importance.

Premium: A periodic, regular payment you must pay for your insurance coverage. Premiums are usually paid in installments.

Prospectus: A document for prospective buyers describing the main features of a mutual fund, stock offering, business venture, and so forth.

Replacement cost or **replacement value:** Amount it will currently cost you to replace an item.

Résumé: A written summary of your work experience, education, and accomplishments used to obtain an employment interview.

Return: Annual percentage amount reflecting the gain or loss on a total amount invested.

Returned check: A check that your financial institution does not pay because you do not have enough money in your account to cover the amount of the check.

Rider or floater: An amendment or addition to a contract or insurance policy.

Securities: An investment instrument—usually stock and bond certificates.

Security deposit: Money held by your landlord during the term of your rental agreement to offset any damages incurred due to your actions.

Sublease: A lease granted by a person already leasing that property.

Surcharges: Charges in addition to another.

Tax return: Form used to provide the Internal Revenue Service with your taxable income information.

Tax schedule: Forms filed with your tax return to supply supporting information.

W-2 Form: The form you may receive from your employer that indicates the total amount of money earned in a calendar year and also the total amount of taxes withheld from those earnings. This form comes with several copies, one each to be filed with your federal, state, and local (if any) returns, as well as a copy for your records.

W-4 Form: The form your employer uses to determine the amount of taxes to be withheld from your wages. You fill out the form by indicating your Social Security number and how many personal exemptions or dependents you which to claim.

Withholding: The amount of your income that your employer sends to the federal, state, and local tax authorities as partial payment of your tax liability.

Bibliography

Baldrige, Letitia. *Letitia Baldrige's New Complete Guide to Executive Manners*. New York: Rawson Associates, 1993.

———. *Letitia Baldrige's New Manners for New Times—A Complete Guide to Etiquette*. New York: Scribner, 2003.

Bernstein, Amy D., and Peter W. Bernstein, eds. *The New York Times Practical Guide to Practically Everything*. New York: St. Martin's Press, 2009.

Bernstein, Mark W. and Yadin Kaufmann. *How to Survive Your Freshman Year*. Atlanta, Georgia: Hundreds of Heads Books LLC.; 2013.

Brody, Lora. *The Kitchen Survival Guide*. New York: William Morrow and Company, Inc., 1992.

Eischen, Clifford W., and Lynn A. Eischen. *Résumés, Cover Letters, Networking, and Interviewing*. Mason, Ohio: South-Western College Pub; 2012.

Eisenberg, Ronni with Kate Kelly. *Organize Yourself!* New York: Collier Books, 2005.

Fireside, Bryna J. *Choices for the High School Graduate: A Survival Guide for the Information Age*. New York: Checkmark Books, 2009.

Forni, P. M. *Choosing Civility—The Twenty-five Rules of Considerate Conduct*. New York: St. Martin's Press, 2003.

Friedman, Jack P. *Dictionary of Business Terms*. New York: Barrons, 2012.

Hill, Napoleon. *The Law of Success in Sixteen Lessons.* Tribeca Books; 2011.

Hoffman, Ronald L., M.D. *How to Talk With Your Doctor.* Laguna Beach, California: Basic Health Publications, 2011.

Jhung, Paula. *How to Avoid Housework.* New York: Fireside/ Simon and Schuster, 1995.

Johnson, Dorothea. *The Little Book of Etiquette.* Philadelphia: Running Press Miniature Editions, 2010.

Langemeier, Loral. *The Millionaire Maker's Guide to Creating a Cash Machine for Life.* New York: McGraw-Hill; 2007.

Maxwell, John C. *Ethics 101: What Every Leader Needs To Know.* Center Street; 2005.

Orman, Suzy. *The Money Book for the Young, Fabulous & Broke.* New York: River Head Books, 2007.

———. *Women and Money: Owning the Power to Control Your Destiny.* New York: Spiegel and Grau, 2007.

Ripley, Amanda. *The Unthinkable: Who Survives When Disaster Strikes—and Why.* New York: Three Rivers Press; 2009.

Tracy, Brian. *Eat That Frog!: 21 Great Ways to Stop Procrastinating and Get More Done in Less Time.* San Francisco: Koehler Publishers; 2007.

Weil, Andrew. *Eight Weeks to Optimum Health.* New York: Ballantine Books, 2007.

Williams, Art. *Common Sense—A Simple Plan for Financial Independence.* Atlanta: Parklake Publishers, Inc., 1991.

Winston, Stephanie. *Getting Organized.* New York: Grand Central Publishing, 2006.

Index

NOTES

NOTES

Life Skills 101:

A Practical Guide to Leaving Home and Living on Your Own

CHECK YOUR FAVORITE BOOKSTORE OR ORDER HERE

Yes, I'd like _____ copies of Life Skills 101: A Practical Guide to Leaving Home and Living on Your Own @$14.95 each, postage paid.

Name:_____

Address:_____

City:_____ State: ____ Zip: _____

E-mail: _____

Please make your check payable and return to:

Stonewood Publications
P.O. Box Nine
Cortland, Ohio 44410

www.LifeSkills101.com